CLASSIC
FILM
SCRIPTS

LADISLAUS VAJDA, 190L-

PANDORA'S BOX (LULU)

a film by

G. W. Pabst

translated from the German
by Christopher Holme

Simon and Schuster, New York

Published by Simon and Schuster
Rockefeller Center, 630 Fifth Avenue
New York, New York 10020
First printing

General Editor: Sandra Wake

SBN 671-20615-X
Library of Congress Catalog Card Number: 70—119349

This edition is for sale only in the United States of America,
its territories, possessions, protectorates and places mandated to it,
the Philippines and the Dominion of Canada

Manufactured in Great Britain by Villiers Publications Ltd,
London NW5

CONTENTS

A NOTE ON THIS EDITION

This volume contains G. W. Pabst's original shooting script for *Pandora's Box* which was loaned to us by Rudolph Joseph of the Munich Film Archive. As a rule a script does not correspond exactly to the final version of the film but in the case of *Pandora's Box* there were only minor changes. When checking the translation of the German script with the film, we have followed the original style, forgoing actual camera directions, because in a silent film so much technical descriptive matter would have become tedious. Square brackets and footnotes denote the parts of the script that did not appear in the print of the film available for viewing. There is, however, a strong possibility that these scenes were in the original version of the film.

Most of the stills are production stills and therefore do not correspond exactly to the text.

Our thanks are due to Mr. Rudolph Joseph who supplied the script and made his archive collection of stills available to us; to Mr. Harold Nebenzal of Nero Film for permission to publish the script and stills; to Colin Ford of the National Film Archive for loaning a print of the film.

'Pabst and Lulu' by Louise Brooks is reproduced by kind permission of Miss Brooks and *Sight and Sound*, where it first appeared in Summer 1965. Extracts from 'Pabst and the Miracle of Louise Brooks' by Lotte H. Eisner are taken from her book *The Haunted Screen — Expressionism in the German Cinema and the Influence of Max Reinhardt*, and appear with kind permission of Secker & Warburg.

PABST AND LULU

by Louise Brooks

Frank Wedekind's play *Pandora's Box* opens with a prologue. Out of a circus tent steps the Animal Trainer, carrying in his left hand a whip and in his right hand a loaded revolver. 'Walk in,' he says to the audience, 'walk into my menagerie.'

The finest job of casting G. W. Pabst ever did was casting himself as the director, the Animal Trainer of his film adaptation of Wedekind's 'tragedy of monsters.' Never a sentimental trick did this whip hand permit the actors assembled to play his beasts. The revolver he shot straight into the heart of the audience.

As Wedekind wrote and produced *Pandora's Box*, it had been detested, banned and condemned from the 1890's. It was declared to be 'immoral and inartistic.' If, at that time when the sacred pleasures of the ruling class were comparatively private, a play exposing them had called out its dogs of law and censorship feeding on the scraps under the banquet table, how much more savage would be the attack upon a film faithful to Wedekind's text made in 1928 in Berlin, where the ruling class publicly flaunted its pleasures as a symbol of wealth and power. And since nobody truly knows what a director is doing till he is done, nobody connected with the film dreamed that Pabst was risking commercial failure with the story of an 'immoral' prostitute who wasn't crazy about her work, surrounded by the 'inartistic' ugliness of raw bestiality.

Only five years earlier the famous Danish actress Asta Nielsen had condensed Wedekind's play into the moral prostitute film *Loulou*. There was no lesbianism, no incest, Loulou the man-eater devoured her sex victims — Dr. Goll, Schwarz and Schön — and then dropped dead in an acute attack of indigestion. This kind of film, with Pabst improvements, was what audiences were prepared for. Set upon making their disillusionment inescapable, hoping to avoid even my duplication of the straight bob and bangs Nielsen had worn as Loulou, Mr. Pabst tested me with my hair curled. But after seeing the test he gave up this point and left me with my shiny black helmet, except for one curled sequence on the gambling ship.

Besides daring to film Wedekind's problem of abnormal psychology — 'this fatal destiny which is the subject of the tragedy'; besides daring to show the prostitute as the victim; Mr. Pabst went on to the final damning immorality of making his Lulu as 'sweetly innocent' as the flowers which adorned her costumes and filled the scenes of the play. 'Lulu is not a real character,' Wedekind said, 'but the personification of primitive sexuality who inspires evil unaware. She plays a purely passive role.' In the middle of the prologue, dressed in her boy's costume of Pierrot, she is *carried* by a stage hand before the Animal Trainer, who tells her, '. . . Be unaffected, and not pieced out with distorted, artificial folly, even if the critics praise you for it less wholly. And mind — all foolery and making faces, the childish simpleness of vice disgraces.'

This was the Lulu, when the film was released, whom the critics praised not less wholly, but not at all. 'Louise Brooks cannot act. She does not suffer. She does nothing.' So far as they were concerned, Pabst had shot a blank. It was I who was struck down by my failure, although he had done everything possible to protect and strengthen me against this deadly blow. He never again allowed me to be publicly identified with the film after the night during production when we appeared as guests at the opening of an UFA film. Leaving the Gloria Palast, as he hurried me through a crowd of hostile fans, I heard a girl saying something loud and nasty. In the cab I began pounding his knee, insisting, 'What did she say? What did she say?' until he translated: 'That is the American girl who is playing our German Lulu.'

In the studio, with that special, ubiquitous sense penetrating minds and walls alike, Mr. Pabst put down all overt acts of contempt. Although I never complained, he substituted another for the assistant who woke me out of my dressing-room naps, beating the door, bellowing, 'Fräulein Brooks! Come!' The subtler forms of my humiliation he assuaged with his own indifference to human regard. Using his strength I learned to block off painful impressions. Sitting on the set day after day, my darling maid Josephine, who had worked for Asta Nielsen and thought she was the greatest actress in the world, came to love me tenderly because I was the world's worst actress. For the same reason, the great actor Fritz Kortner never spoke to me at all. He, like everybody else on the production, thought I had cast some blinding spell over Mr. Pabst

6

which allowed me to walk through my part. To them it was a sorry outcome of Pabst's search for Lulu, about which one of his assistants, Paul Falkenberg, said in 1955 : ' Preparation for *Pandora's Box* was quite a saga, because Pabst couldn't find a Lulu. He wasn't satisfied with any actress at hand and for months everybody connected with the production went around looking for a Lulu. I talked to girls on the street, on the subway, in railway stations — " Would you mind coming up to our office? I would like to present you to Mr. Pabst." He looked all of them over dutifully and turned them all down. And eventually he picked Louise Brooks.'

How Pabst determined that I was his unaffected Lulu with the childish simpleness of vice was part of the mysterious alliance that seemed to exist between us even before we met. He knew nothing more of me than an unimportant part he saw me play in the Howard Hawks film *A Girl in Every Port*. I had never heard of him, and knew nothing of his unsuccessful negotiations to borrow me from Paramount until I was called to the front office on the option day of my contract. Ben Schulberg told me that I could stay on at my old salary or quit. It was the time of the switch-over to talkies and studios were cutting actors' salaries just for the hell of it. And, just for the hell of it, I quit. Then he told me about the Pabst offer, which I was now free to accept. I said I would accept it and he sent off a cable to Pabst. All this took about ten minutes and left Schulberg somewhat dazed by my composure and quick decision.

But if I had not acted at once I would have lost the part of Lulu. At that very hour in Berlin Marlene Dietrich was waiting with Pabst in his office. ' Dietrich was too old and too obvious — one sexy look and the picture would become a burlesque. But I gave her a deadline and the contract was about to be signed when Paramount cabled saying I could have Louise Brooks.' It must be remembered that Pabst was speaking about the pre-von Sternberg Dietrich. She was the Dietrich of *I Kiss Your Hand, Madame*, a film in which, caparisoned variously in beads, brocade, ostrich feathers, chiffon ruffles and white rabbit fur, she galloped from one lascivious stare to another. Years after another trick of fate had made her a top star — for Sternberg's biographer Herman Weinberg told me that it was only because Brigitte Helm was not available that he looked further and found Dietrich for *The Blue Angel* — to Travis Banton, the Paramount dress designer who transformed her spangles and feathers into glittering shadowed beauty, she said : ' Imagine Pabst choosing Louise Brooks for Lulu when he could have had me ! '

So it is that my playing of the tragic Lulu with no sense of sin remains generally unacceptable to this day. Three years ago, after seeing *Pandora's Box* at Eastman House, a priest said to me, ' How did you feel? playing — *that girl!* ' ' Feel? I felt fine ! It all seemed perfectly normal to me.' Seeing him start with distaste and disbelief, and unwilling to be mistaken for one of those women who like to shock priests with sensational confessions, I went on to prove the truth of Lulu's world by my own experience in the 1925 *Follies*, when my best friend was a lesbian and I knew two millionaire publishers, much like Schön in the film, who backed shows to keep themselves well supplied with Lulus. But the priest rejected my reality exactly as Berlin had rejected its reality when we made *Lulu* and sex was the business of the town.

At the Eden Hotel where I lived the café bar was lined with the better-priced trollops. The economy girls walked the street outside. On the corner stood the girls in boots advertising flagellation. Actors' agents pimped for the ladies in luxury apartments in the Bavarian Quarter. Racetrack touts at the Hoppegarten arranged orgies for groups of sportsmen. The night club Eldorado displayed an enticing line of homosexuals dressed as women. At the Maly there was a choice of feminine or collar-and-tie lesbians. Collective lust roared unashamed at the theatre. In the revue *Chocolate Kiddies*, when Josephine Baker appeared naked except for a girdle of bananas, it was precisely as Lulu's stage entrance was described. ' They rage there as in a menagerie when the meat appears at the cage.'

I revered Pabst for his truthful picture of this world of pleasure which let me play Lulu naturally. The rest of the cast were tempted to rebellion. And perhaps that was his most brilliant directorial achievement — getting a group of actors to play characters without ' sympathy ', whose only motivation was sexual gratification. Fritz Kortner as Schön wanted to be the victim. Franz Lederer as the incestuous son Alwa Schön wanted to be adorable. Carl Götz wanted to get laughs playing the old pimp Schigolch. Alice Roberts, the Belgian actress who played the screen's first lesbian, the Countess Geschwitz, was prepared to go no further than repression in mannish suits.

8

Her first day's work was in the wedding sequence. She came on the set looking chic in her Paris evening dress and aristocratically self-possessed. Then Mr. Pabst began explaining the action of the scene in which she was to dance the tango with me. Suddenly she understood that she was to touch, to embrace, to make love to another woman. Her blue eyes bulged and her hands trembled. Anticipating the moment of explosion, Mr. Pabst, who proscribed unscripted emotional outbursts, caught her arm and sped her away out of sight behind the set. A half-hour later when they returned, he was hissing soothingly to her in French and she was smiling like the star of the picture . . . which she was in all her scenes with me. I was just there obstructing the view. In both two-shots and her close-ups photographed over my shoulder she cheated her look past me to Mr. Pabst making love to her off camera. Out of the funny complexity of this design Mr. Pabst extracted his tense portrait of sterile lesbian passion and Madame Roberts satisfactorily preserved her reputation. At the time, her conduct struck me as silly. The fact that the public could believe an actress's private life to be like one role in one film did not come home to me till last year when I was visited by a French boy. Explaining why the young people in Paris loved *Lulu*, he put an uneasy thought in my mind. ' You talk as if I were a lesbian in real life,' I said. ' But of course ! ' he answered in a way that made me laugh to realise I had been living in cinematic perversion for thirty-five years.

Pabst was a short man, broad-shouldered and thick-chested, looking heavy and wilful in repose. But in action his legs carried him on wings which matched the swiftness of his mind. He always came on the set, fresh as a March wind, going directly to the camera to check the set-up, after which he turned to his cameraman Günther Krampf, who was the only person on the film to whom he gave a complete account of the scene's action and meaning. Never conducting group discussions with his actors, he then took each separately to be told what he must know about the scene. To Pabst, the carry-over of the acting technique of the theatre, which froze in advance every word, every move, every emotion, was death to realism in films. He wanted the shocks of life which released unpredictable emotions. Proust wrote : ' Our life is at every moment before us like a stranger in the night, and which of us knows what point he will reach on the morrow ? ' To prevent actors from plotting every point they would make on the morrow, Pabst never quite shot the scenes they prepared for.

On the day we shot Lulu's murder of Schön, Fritz Kortner came on the set with his death worked out to the last facial contortion; with even his blood, the chocolate syrup which would ooze from his mouth, carefully tested for sweetness lest it might surprise an unrehearsed reaction. Death scenes are dearer than life to the actor, and Kortner's, spectacularly coloured with years of theatrical dying, went unquestioned during rehearsal. Pabst left it to the mechanics of each shot to alter Kortner's performance. The smoke from the firing of the revolver became of first importance, or the exact moment when Kortner pulled my dress off my shoulder, or the photographic consistency of the chocolate syrup — all such technical irritations broke a series of prepared emotions into unhinged fragments of reality.

Dialogue was set by Pabst while he watched the actors during rehearsal. In an effort to be funny, old actors and directors have spread the false belief that any clownish thing coming to mind could be said in front of the camera in silent films. They forget the title writer had to match his work to the actors' speech. I remember late one night wandering into Ralph Spence's suite in the Beverly Wilshire, where he sat gloomily amidst cans of film, cartons of stale Chinese food and empty whisky bottles. He was trying to fix up an unfunny Beery and Hatton comedy and no comic line he invented would fit the lip action. Silent film fans were excellent lip-readers and often complained at the box-office about the cowboy cussing furiously trying to mount his horse. Besides which, directors like Pabst used exact dialogue to isolate and intensify an emotion. When Lulu was looking down at the dead Schön, he gave me the line, ' Das Blut ! ' Not the murder of my husband but the sight of the blood determined the expression on my face.

That I was a dancer, and Pabst essentially a choreographer in his direction, came as a wonderful surprise to both of us on the first day of shooting *Pandora's Box*. The expensive English translation of the script which I had thrown unopened on the floor by my chair, had already been retrieved by an outraged assistant and banished with Mr. Pabst's laughter. Consequently I did not know that Lulu was a professional dancer trained in Paris — ' Gipsy, oriental, skirt dance ', or that dancing was her mode of expression

10

— 'In my despair I dance the Can-Can!' On the afternoon of that first day Pabst said to me, 'In this scene Schigolch rehearses you in a dance number.' After marking out a small space and giving me a fast tempo, he looked at me curiously. 'You can make up some little steps here — can't you?' I nodded yes and he walked away. It was a typical instance of his care in protecting actors against the blight of failure. If I had been able to do nothing more than the skippity-hops of Asta Nielsen his curious look would never have been amplified to regret, although the intensity of his concern was revealed by his delight when the scene was finished. As I was leaving the set he caught me in his arms, shaking me and laughing as if I had played a joke on him. 'But you are a professional dancer!' It was the moment when he realised all his intuitions about me were right. He felt as if he had created me. I was his Lulu! The bouquet of roses he gave me on my arrival at the Station am Zoo was my first and last experience of the deference he applied to the other actors. From that moment I was firmly put through my tricks with no fish thrown in for a good performance.

Four days later I was less wonderfully surprised when he also subjected my private life to his direction. His delight in Lulu's character belonged exclusively to the film. Off the screen my dancing days came to an end when a friend of mine from Washington, with whom I had been investigating Berlin's night life till three every morning, left for Paris. On the set the next day I had just accepted an invitation to an 'Artists' Ball — Wow!' when Mr. Pabst's quiet, penetrating voice sounded behind me. 'Pretzfelder! Loueees does not go out any more at night.' Pretzfelder melted away as I began to howl in protest, 'But Mr. Pabst, I have always gone out at night when I worked! I can catch up on my sleep between scenes here at the studio. I always have!' He didn't hear me because he was busy laying down the law to Josephine, who thereafter, when the day's work was done, returned his Eve to the Eden where I was bathed, fed and put to bed till called for next morning at seven. Cross and restless, I was left to fall asleep listening to the complaints of the other poor caged beasts across Stresemann-Strasse in the Zoologischer Garten.

In the matter of my costumes for the picture I put up a better fight, although I never won a decision. My best punches fanned the air because Pabst had always slipped into another position. Arriving in Berlin on Sunday and starting the picture on the following Wednesday, I found he had selected my first costume, leaving me nothing to do but stand still for a final fitting. This I let pass as an expedient, never suspecting it would be the same with everything else I put on or took off, from an ermine coat to my girdle. Not only was it unheard of to allow an actress no part in choosing her clothes, but I had also been disgustingly spoiled by my directors at Paramount. I had played a manicurist in 500-dollar beaded evening dresses; a salesgirl in 300-dollar black satin afternoon dresses; and a schoolgirl in 250-dollar tailored suits. (It tickles me today when people see these old pictures and wonder why I look so well and the other girls such frumps.)

With this gross over-confidence in my rights and power, I had defied Mr. Pabst at first with arrogance. The morning of the sequence in which I was to go from my bath into a love scene with Franz Lederer, I came on the set wrapped in a gorgeous négligée of painted yellow silk. Carrying the peignoir I refused to wear, Josephine approached Mr. Pabst to receive the lash. Hers was the responsibility for seeing that I obeyed his orders, and he answered her excuses with a stern rebuke. Then he turned to me. ' Loueees, you must wear the peignoir! ' ' Why? I hate that big old woolly white bathrobe! ' ' Because,' he said, ' the audience must know you are naked beneath it.' Stunned by such a reasonable argument, without another word I retired with Josephine to the bathroom set and changed into the peignoir.

Not to be trapped in this manner again, when I objected to the train of my wedding dress being ' tied on like an apron ' and he explained that it had to be easily discarded because I could not play a long, frantic sequence tripping over my train, I answered that I did not give a damn, tore off the train and went into an elaborate tantrum. The worst audience I ever had, Mr. Pabst instructed the dress designer to have the pieces sewn together again and left the fitting room. My final defeat, crying real tears, came at the end of the picture when he went through my trunks to select a dress to be ' aged ' for Lulu's murder as a streetwalker in the arms of Jack the Ripper. With his instinctive understanding of my tastes, he decided on the blouse and skirt of my very favourite suit. I was anguished. ' Why can't you *buy* some cheap little dress to be ruined? Why does it have to be *my* dress? ' To these questions I got no

12

answer till the next morning, when my once lovely clothes were returned to me in the studio dressing-room. They were torn and foul with grease stains. Not some indifferent rags from the wardrobe department, but my own suit which only last Sunday I had worn to lunch at the Adlon! Josephine hooked up my skirt, I slipped the blouse over my head and went on the set feeling as hopelessly defiled as my clothes.

Dancing for two years with Ruth St. Denis and Ted Shawn had taught me much about the magic worked with authentic costuming. Their most popular duet, *Tillers of the Soil*, was costumed in potato sacking. In her *Flower Arrangement*, Miss Ruth's magnificent Japanese robes did most of the dancing. But the next three years of uncontrolled extravagance in films had so corrupted my judgment that I did not realise until I saw *Pandora's Box* in 1956 how marvellously Mr. Pabst's perfect costume sense symbolised Lulu's character and her destruction. There is not a single spot of blood on the pure white bridal satin in which she kills her husband. Making love to her wearing the clean white peignoir, Alwa asks, ' Do you love me, Lulu? ' ' I? Never a soul! ' It is in the worn and filthy garments of the streetwalker that she feels passion for the first time — comes to life so that she may die. When she picks up Jack the Ripper on the foggy London street and he tells her he has no money to pay her, she says, ' Never mind, I like you.' It is Christmas Eve and she is about to receive the gift which has been her dream since childhood. Death by a sexual maniac.

PABST AND THE MIRACLE OF LOUISE BROOKS

by Lotte H. Eisner

In the English review *Close Up*, which so ardently championed Pabst's films in the thirties, a critic claimed that ' Pabst finds the other side of each woman '. This is obviously true in the case of Brigitte Helm, for example, frigid as the two Marias in Lang's *Metropolis* and so moving in Pabst's *Love of Jeanne Ney*. But how was it that for *Abwege* or *Herrin von Atlantis* Pabst failed to warm the impenetrable beauty of this actress, who is as insensitive in these two films as in the title role in both versions of *Alraune*?

But in *Pandora's Box* and *Diary of a Lost Girl* we have the miracle of Louise Brooks. Her gifts of profound intuition may seem purely passive to an inexperienced audience, yet she succeeded in stimulating an otherwise unequal director's talent to the extreme. Pabst's remarkable evolution must thus be seen as an encounter with an actress who needed no directing, but could move across the screen causing the work of art to be born by her mere presence. Louise Brooks, always enigmatically impassive, overwhelmingly exists throughout these two films. We know now that Louise Brooks is a remarkable actress endowed with uncommon intelligence, and not merely a dazzlingly beautiful woman.

Pandora's Box is a silent film. As such it does very well without the words which Wedekind — the author of the two plays *Erdgeist* and *Die Büchse der Pandora*, which Pabst condensed into one film — deemed indispensable to bring out the erotic power of this singular ' earthly being ' endowed with animal beauty, but lacking all moral sense, and doing evil unconsciously . . .

The editing of *Pandora's Box* is more fluid [than some of his other films], perhaps because Pabst's weakness for fluctuating atmosphere or violently-contrasted chiaroscuro (the lighted boat at night) comes to the fore. Despite this stylistic fluidity the fusion of two stage-plays leads to certain passages in the film standing out from the whole, as was noted by one of the *Close Up* critics. Each composes a drama in its own right, with its own peripetias, rhythm and style distinct from the rest. Such self-contained sequences are the Impressionistic glitter of the revue scenes, the Expressionistically lit gambling-hell on the boat, and the foggy images of London low-life.

Nobody has ever equalled Pabst's portrayal of the back-stage fever on the opening night of a big show, the hurrying and scurrying during the scene changes, the stage seen from the wings as the performers go on and off and bound forward to acknowledge their applause at the end of their act, the rivalry, complacency, and humour, the bewildering bustle of stage-hands and electricians — a stupendous whirl of artistic aspirations, colourful detail, and a facile eroticism. Even the famous *42nd Street* does not get across this dazzle and warmth, this sensuality swamped in the light shim-

14

mering on the lamé curtains and the helmets and suits of armour, and silvering the bodies of the all-but-naked women. Pabst directs all this turmoil with remarkable dexterity; everything has been worked out in advance; at precisely calculated intervals a few figures cross in front of or behind a main group, giving an impression of effervescence and dynamism. Lulu appears like some pagan idol, tempting, glittering with spangles, feathers, and frills, against a wavering, out-of-focus background.

She is the centre of attraction, and Pabst succeeds in devising an infinite variety of seduction scenes to show her to advantage, as when Dr. Schön comes into the flat wondering how to tell his mistress that he is getting married. The camera catches his nervousness as he paces up and down the room; the ash from his cigarette burns a table-runner, and he fiddles with a bibelot, as Jannings had fidgeted with a liqueur glass in *Variety*. Then a skilful shot-and-reverse shot shows us Lulu observing him. She sinks back into the cushions, moves, lies on her front half-reared like a sphinx, while Schön goes up to her and sits down. The camera dives and scrutinizes Lulu's impassive features, lingering over the perfect sweep of her face, the pearl-like quality of her skin, the fringe of her lacquered hair, the sharp arch of her eyebrows, and the trembling shadow of her lashes.

Another passage offers a subtle variant : in the prop-room Lulu throws herself on to the divan, and the camera moves up to the white nape of her neck and slips along her legs as they kick with impatience. The two lovers wrestle and sink into a long embrace. These scenes are extremely erotic, but quite free from vulgarity.

Many times Pabst films Lulu's features on a slant. Her face is so voluptuously animal that it seems almost deprived of individuality. In the scene with Jack the Ripper, this face, a smooth mirror-like disc slanting across the screen, is so shaded out and toned down that the camera seems to be looking down at some lunar landscape. (Is this still a human being — a woman — at all? Is it not rather the flower of some poisonous plant?) Or again Pabst just shows, at the edge of the screen, the chin and a fragment of cheek belonging to the man next to her, with whom the audience automatically identifies.

In the final episode, in the London slum, she uses the reflector of the lamp as a mirror with which to apply her lipstick. Jack the

15

Ripper gets the idea of using the bread-knife from seeing it glint in the light of this same lamp. His face stands out from the half-light in full relief, a tragic counterpoise to the smooth features of the beloved Lulu. For a brief moment the haunted man smiles and the veil of despair seems to lift from his suddenly appeased features. Then the camera immediately reveals again each bump in the skin; each pore is visible, and the sweat over the contracted muscles.

It is the close-ups which determine the character of the film; the flamboyant or phosphorescent atmosphere and the luminous mists of London remain throughout merely a kind of accompaniment to these close-ups, heightening their significance.

Pabst introduces a character with a single shot: scrutinizing the acrobat Rodrigo waiting in the street, the camera lingers over his square shoulders and barrel chest; in this shot his head has become a mere accessory, and we immediately realize that the man is brainless, nothing but physical strength.

As soon as Lulu's adoptive father make his appearance on the landing Pabst shows us his hunched silhouette from behind, and this stresses the sordid aspect of the debauched old artiste's way of life.

Sometimes Pabst can indicate all the drama in a single shot: Lulu, wearing the wedding-dress, looks at herself in the mirror and then leans forward to put down her pearl necklace; while she does so, and her image leaves the mirror, the threatening figure of Dr. Schön is framed in the glass. Lulu straightens up, and her image meets that of Dr. Schön, who has decided to kill her. Pabst then cuts very briefly to the struggle for the revolver; Lulu is seen from behind, we perceive a puff of smoke and realize that the gun has gone off. Then we have all the details of Schön's death throes, shown from dramatic angles. . . .

To sum up the elements of Pabst's technique: he seeks the ' psychological or dramatic angles ' which reveal at a single glance character, psychical relationships, situations, tension, or the tragic moment. Most of the time he prefers this method of shooting to Murnau's technique of following a scene at length with a moving camera. So, for Pabst, the action is ultimately built up by the montage.

16

CREDITS:

Screenplay by	Ladislaus Vajda from two plays by Frank Wedekind, *Erdgeist* and *Die Büchse der Pandora*
Directed by	G. W. Pabst
Produced by	George C. Horsetzky
Production company	Nero Film A.G.
Director of photography	Günther Krampf
Art director	Andrei Andreiev
Costumes by	Gottlieb Hesch
Assistant directors	Mark Sorkin, Paul Falkenberg
Edited by	Joseph R. Fliesler
Process	Black and white
Length	3,254 metres
Running time	131 minutes
First shown in Berlin	February 1929

CAST:

Lulu	Louise Brooks
Dr. Peter Schön	Fritz Kortner
Alwa Schön, his son	Franz Lederer
Schigolch (Papa Brommer)	Carl Götz
Countess Anna Geschwitz	Alice Roberts
Marie de Zarniko	Daisy d'Ora
Rodrigo Quast	Krafft Raschig
Marquis Casti-Piani	Michael von Newlinsky
The Stage Manager	Siegfried Arno
Jack the Ripper	Gustav Diessl

17

PANDORA'S BOX (LULU)

Fade in from credits to the Hall of Lulu's Own Little Apartment. In a corner in front of the electricity meter a company Official is standing taking the reading. [But clearly he has not quite got his mind on the job; he keeps glancing sideways at a door.]*

Lulu now comes through it, fumbling in her handbag for the money to pay the Official. (Still on page 33)** She is wearing a négligée which she has not done up at all carefully, and she has a liqueur bottle wedged under her arm. She smiles and approaches the Official. He has his back to her and steadily goes on with his work as Lulu comes up behind him.

Smiling impishly, she starts to pour out a small glass of liqueur for him.

The Official beams at her, and at the drink.

As she fills the little glass to the brim, Lulu smiles engagingly at the Official. Then she wedges the bottle back under her arm, puts a serious expression on her face and takes the bill in one hand; then she smiles again as she hands the Official his drink with her other hand.

While the Official is happily emptying his glass, Lulu gravely checks the bill, takes her handbag from under her arm and, very importantly, counts what she has to pay from her purse and gives it to him. He does not know whether to look at what the négligée reveals or the bottle of liqueur. Indeed, he is so confused that some of Lulu's coins roll to the floor without his noticing. His confusion has reached such a pitch that possibly the icy armour of his official dignity might melt away altogether, if there was not a ring at the door bell.

A shabbily dressed man is standing with his back to us on the landing

---

* This is not entirely clear from the film, in which the Official is intent on his work and does not look sideways.

** At this point in Pabst's original script preserved in the Munich Archive, there is a reference to another opening to the film. The script states that 'Lulu is changed and has her hair done differently, and we feel at once that she has taken great trouble with her appearance and has largely succeeded in obliterating her past as a flower girl. Outwardly, she has become a real little lady.' The opening scenes of Lulu's life before she met Dr. Schön have been deleted from the surviving script and from all extant prints of the film.

outside Lulu's little apartment.

Lulu is about to go and answer the door, but the Official ceremoniously stops her and jumps to answer it for her.

At the door, giving a low sweep of his hat as a greeting, stands Schigolch.

Seeing this little old man in the baggy suit and worn, greasy hat, the Official begins to select a coin from the money left in his hand and offers it to the presumed beggar.

Lulu is straining her neck to see who is at the door. She recognises the old man, and with a delighted cry of ' Papa Brommer !' jumps with excitement and dashes to the door.

The old man, also, is wild with excitement as she boisterously embraces him and pulls him into the room. Without taking any notice of the meter man, she drags Schigolch imperiously across the hall and flings him ecstatically into the sitting-room.

The Official stands bewildered, speechless, as the door is shut on him. An illusion is destroyed. All at once he notices that he has lost some money; his face resumes the frown of officialdom, he kneels down . . .

And picks up two fallen coins from the floor. Then, as camera pans to a chair beside him, he leans across and takes his briefcase from it. He stuffs it firmly under his arm, puts his cap on his head, and with a final indignant nod at the closed door, marches stiffly out. Fade out.

[Lulu's Bedroom is bright and wispily furnished. Lulu stands with Schigolch in the middle of the room, showing him, with childlike pleasure, the bed, the dressing-table. She drags him over to the wardrobe, which she throws open to display the many dresses hanging up in it. She takes out one or two of them and holds them in front of her to show Schigolch what lovely things she now possesses. Schigolch looks at everything with interest, and at the liqueur bottle which Lulu is still holding under her arm. She hasn't taken the time to put it down. He reaches for it in a businesslike way, smells it, then takes a big gulp direct out of the bottle. Lulu has thrown the dress over the bed, takes Schigolch by the arm, and drags him out into . . .]*

---

* This scene taken from the original script did not appear in the version screened. In the film itself, Lulu flings Schigolch straight into the sitting-room from the hall of the apartment.

19

The Sitting-Room, where Lulu seizes Schigolch and they spin each other right round with childlike exuberance.

Lulu stands back smiling proudly, her hands on her hips, so as to show off the beautifully furnished room.

Schigolch, leaning on the mantelpiece and taking off his gloves, looks round at it all with a certain scepticism.

She laughs, exasperated. It is as if he hasn't understood. ' It's mine !' she seems to say, clutching her hands to her breast.

But he is still sceptical and not swept away by Lulu's excitement. Putting his gloves on the mantelpiece behind him, he notices Lulu's purse lying there. So he picks it up and takes out a roll of notes and, casually licking his fingers, starts to count them.

Lulu's smile changes to a frown.

Schigolch helps himself to some of the bills, then puts the rest back in the purse, and the purse back on the shelf.

Lulu cannot be angry at him; she throws back her head and laughs . . .

As Schigolch says :

TITLE : *You've made a lot of progress.*

He sits down in an easy chair, drawing Lulu onto his lap. She flings her arms round his neck and hugs him excitedly, and while he strokes and fondles her, he says :

TITLE : *It's a long time since we last met.*

Lulu hugs him and they rock gently back and forth. (Still on page 34) Schigolch's glance falls on . . .

The liqueur bottle standing on the side table.

His eyes brighten as he takes it up and Lulu eagerly offers to get him a glass, but no, Schigolch will just take the pourer out of the top and drink it straight from the bottle; it is quicker that way.

Lulu pretends to disapprove, just for a moment, then changes her mind : no, he must take as much as he wants.

So Schigolch lifts the bottle to his lips and takes a long gulp. It makes him feel good and Lulu is happy that he is happy. He smiles his thanks and approval. Then Schigolch looks over at . . .

A painting of Lulu, dressed as a harlequin and holding a stringed instrument, which hangs on the opposite wall.

He says to her :

TITLE : *Do you still dance?*

She protests that she doesn't, but Schigolch insists and pushes her off his lap to dance for him.
So she leaps up exuberantly and runs across the room . . .
To stand in front of her picture, where she begins to fling her arms around in an ecstatic dance.
Schigolch, meanwhile, is unwrapping a mouth organ which he has taken from his pocket.
And as Lulu dances, flinging her arms and legs wildly and pirouetting in the lovely flowing négligée . . . (Still on page 34)
He plays along with her on his mouth organ, beating out a tune . . .
She turns and turns. Suddenly she stops uncertainly. She cannot dance to the tune.
Schigolch whips the mouth organ down from his lips. He is furious. His sudden rage frightens Lulu. Nervously, she tries to start dancing again.
But Schigolch has had enough; he is too angry. He leaps from the chair . . .
And storms across to her, brandishing the mouth organ as if he is going to strike her. Lulu cowers beneath him in fright. But his anger dies as quickly as it rose, and he even smiles as he says :

TITLE : *You've forgotten everything. You'd have done better to stay with me.*

Lulu throws her head back and laughs with relief :

TITLE : *In that attic? I'd have run away from there for sure.*

In spite of himself Schigolch has to agree; she's certainly better off at the moment :

TITLE : *Schön and his newspapers will look after you all right, but having a friend like that won't always pay the rent.*

Lulu looks at him questioningly. She doesn't understand what he's getting at. Schigolch continues :

TITLE : *You must be introduced to a wider public. I've brought just the man with me, somebody who'll help you on in your career.*

Schigolch [looks towards the balcony door, which is open] stands up

21

and goes out with Lulu on to . . .

The Balcony, where he leans out over the balustrade, looks down into the street and there shows Lulu . . .

A man, tall, powerful, looking like an athlete, who is walking up and down outside the house.

Schigolch says to Lulu :

TITLE : *It's Rodrigo Quast. He wants to do a big Variety turn with you.*

He is just about to beckon to the man . . .

Now waiting impatiently by a lamp-post . . . (Still on page 34)

To come up, when Lulu holds back his arm and listens. She pulls him away from the balustrade :

TITLE : *Dr. Schön's coming.*

Hastily she pushes Schigolch onto the floor in a corner of the balcony and dashes back into the apartment.

In the Hall, Dr. Schön is just coming through the door which he has opened with his own key. He shuts the door and puts the key in his pocket.

Going across to the coat rack, he takes off his topcoat and puts it, with his bowler hat, onto a peg.

On the Balcony, Schigolch is waving an arm anxiously at Lulu. She comes flying back with his bowler hat and gloves, and, most important of all, the bottle of liqueur. Schigolch, quickly understanding what's going on, makes himself comfortable in this hiding-place, which he finds all the easier now because of the bottle which he has by him.

Lulu hurries back into . . .

The Sitting-Room, where Dr. Schön is already coming to meet her. Lulu is radiant as she spreads out both her arms . . .

And leaps across to him, taking him in her usual loving caress. But Dr. Schön stands morosely before her, merely submitting to this extravagant display of affection. (Still on page 34)

Out on the Balcony, something seems to be bothering Schigolch; he shifts about uneasily.

In the Sitting-Room, Dr. Schön strokes Lulu's arm with a fleeting gesture of tenderness, then turns abruptly and goes across the room. Lulu lets her arms fall and looks at him with astonishment. She follows him with her eyes as . . .

He paces the room from side to side. He sits down heavily on the arm of the easy chair, keeping his back to Lulu.

She watches him, frowning now, as . . .

His hand toys nervously with a little porcelain ornament on the mantelpiece. He turns the little animal round and round as . . .

Lulu looks at him out of the corner of her eye.

His hand lets the little ornament fall back to its place. He gets up, turns to face her, starts to speak but cannot go through with it. He paces the room as . . .

Lulu's eyes follow him.

Again he stops, looks up at her sideways, but cannot bring himself to declare his terrible news. He sighs and bites his lip in despair, and starts pacing again.

Lulu, watching him from beneath her eyelids, lets a confident little smile form at the corners of her mouth.

Dr. Schön, in his restless pacing, has reached the divan in front of Lulu's portrait. Taking a cigarette from Lulu's box on the side table and putting it in his lips, he slowly sits down.

Lulu smiles knowingly.

As he lights the cigarette . . .

Lulu is already laughing. She comes up to him, her head on one side in a question.

Without looking up at her, he announces :

TITLE : *I'm going to get married!*

Lulu laughs aloud with relief and flings both her arms round his neck, saying :

TITLE : *And is that why you don't kiss me, because you want to get married?*

Dr. Schön frees himself from Lulu's arms and escapes once more to the balcony side of the room.

Lulu follows him with her eyes . . .

And then stretches herself out provocatively on the divan . . .

Where she lies, her chin resting on her cupped hands, waiting. (Still on page 34)

Dr. Schön goes over to the balcony window and lights another cigarette. His hard-won resolution is beginning to waver in the face of Lulu's smiling certainty.

She looks over at him coquettishly.

He puffs gloomily on his cigarette for a while . . .

Then drops it onto the balcony floor beside a potted plant. It smoulders there.

With sudden determination he takes his monocle from his right eye, swings round, and paces back to . . .

Lulu, stretched out on her side on the divan. She turns languidly over onto her back, her arms inviting him to come to her. In a despairing outburst he says:

TITLE: *Our affair is the talk of the whole town. I'm ruining my career!*

Dr. Schön's outburst makes no impression at all on Lulu. She only reaches up to him again.

He sits morosely beside her, brooding.

She pulls him, only weakly resisting, down to her, winding her arms about his neck. [Dr. Schön makes one more attempt to get free. He drags himself upright, but since Lulu has wound her arms firmly around his neck, he pulls her up with him. And when he doesn't succeed in shaking off Lulu's embrace, his resistance finally collapses; in a frenzy of passion he clasps her to him and, while he holds Lulu's body entwined in his, he groans:

TITLE: *Don't you understand that we must end it?*

Lulu's only reply is to snuggle with her cheek against his face, as she smiles childishly and sweetly, speaking softly past his ear:]

TITLE: *You'll have to kill me if you want to get rid of me.**

Conquered, once more under Lulu's spell, Dr. Schön allows her to pull him onto the divan. Once more he tries to free himself and get up, only to fall back onto her all the more passionately. For a while nothing is seen of the two; they have passed out of the picture, back down onto the divan.

On the Balcony, Schigolch is still bundled in the corner, the liqueur bottle in one hand. He takes a long gulp out of it.

A little lap-dog, sleeping by the potted plant, wakes up, pricks his

---

* In the National Film Archive print, this title card appears immediately after Lulu has put her arms round Dr. Schön's neck.

24

ears and looks around. He cocks his ear in the direction of the room, then he moves and turns his head to where . . .

Schigolch is squatting in his corner, bottle in hand, trying to give the dog a friendly smile.

But the dog doesn't want to be friends with this scarecrow and starts yelping loudly.

Schigolch is nervous and covers his face with his hat, horrified at the noise the dog is making.

In the Sitting-Room, Lulu, deep in Schön's arms, suddenly awakens from the languor of his caress and puts her head up to listen.

Out on the Balcony, the dog will not stop yelping.

Schigolch tries to make friends with the little dog.

Lulu laughs unrestrainedly, jumps up, [breaks loose from the astonished Schön and runs out onto] . . .

The Balcony, where Schigolch is trying desperately to pacify the dog. He pours some liqueur into his hand and offers it to the dog. [The remedy seems to work, because the dog tries the offered bribe and the barking stops.]

Lulu laughingly coaxes the little dog, which now again starts barking ungratefully at Schigolch.

Schigolch is still trying to make friends with the dog; but it turns away and trots towards Lulu.

In the doorway behind Lulu, Dr. Schön now appears.

He stares at . . .

Schigolch, huddled up in his baggy clothes, looking spectral even in bright sunlight, and improbably old. He cowers under Dr. Schön's gaze.

Dr. Schön stares incredulously at the strange sight bundled in the corner of Lulu's balcony.

Lulu, laughing, as if it were a matter of course, points to Schigolch (Still on page 35) and explains to Schön:

TITLE : *That's my first sugar-daddy.*

Dr. Schön can hardly believe his eyes, or his ears.

And as the bundle of old clothes begins to get up, greasy hat on head . . .

Lulu smiles at it . . .

And Schigolch, now standing, lifts his hat in a solemnly courteous manner and remarks, with modest impudence, to the impeccably

25

dressed Dr. Schön:

TITLE: *One did the best that one could.**

Dr. Schön looks in utter horror at Schigolch who . . .
Quite unconcerned, stares back, with a mocking laugh.
Dr. Schön loses his self-control and, without answering, dashes off.
Lulu [puts the dog down on its chair,] laughs, and then rushes out
after Dr. Schön.
In the Hall, Dr. Schön has already snatched his hat from the hook
as Lulu comes and tries to hold him back. But brutally he tears
himself free and leaves the hall, slamming the front door behind
him. Lulu remains, posing herself seductively, and not noticeably
distressed, against the open door.
On the Balcony, Schigolch rushes to the balustrade and leans over
it, gesturing wildly to the man in the street below, telling him to
come up now.
The Street is seen from above. Rodrigo, still waiting down there,
nods joyfully and comes across the street towards the house.
Schigolch leaves the balustrade and heads across the room to meet
him.
Dr. Schön is just coming down the stairs at a furious pace, as
Rodrigo comes through the entrance doorway. Almost at the foot
of the stairs, they pass, each apparently oblivious of the other's
presence. Rodrigo advances ponderously upstairs, while Dr. Schön
storms out through the entrance.
Lulu is still standing in the hall, seductively forlorn, as Schigolch
comes up to say something to her, while pointing to the front door.
He goes over to it . . .
And opens the door.
Lulu stands expectantly, poised.
And soon Rodrigo Quast appears and makes his entrance. Schigolch
takes his arm and brings him forward . . .
Introducing him to Lulu with a friendly word.
Lulu studies him with sympathetic curiosity.
Rodrigo stands there, grinning bashfully.
Lulu gives a little curtsy; Rodrigo bows awkwardly, and Schigolch
looks on. Then Schigolch whips Rodrigo's hat from his head as the
burly man takes Lulu's little hand in his powerful grip. She gasps

---

* In Pabst's original script, it is actually Lulu who says these words.

26

and pulls back, comforting her hand, and amazed at such strength. Rodrigo, beaming proudly at his strength, lifts up his arm to show his biceps to Lulu. (Still on page 35)

She stares in amazement at these powerfully developed muscles. She presses down on them with interest, and exclaims at their hardness. Rodrigo stretches out his arm and with this one movement lifts Lulu from the floor. Merrily she swings herself from this living horizontal bar.

Schigolch grins happily at the little scene.

We see in close-up an invitation card to the wedding of Dr. Schön and the Prime Minister's daughter. It reads:

His Excellency, the Prime Minister
Dr. Zarniko
has the honour to announce the engagement
of his daughter
Charlotte Marie Adelaide
to
Chief Editor
Dr. Peter Schön

In a room in the Prime Minister's house,* the Prime Minister is holding the card. [It is just being put into an envelope. The envelope is sealed and laid on a pile of envelopes, already addressed and lying beside a small typewriter. Now we also see that it is the girl herself who is just taking up another envelope and putting it in the typewriter. We observe, too, that her father is standing beside her.]**

Gravely he leans over to his daughter, the card in his hand, and says urgently:

TITLE: *Once more I warn you, my child. Dr. Schön's behaviour*

---

* In the original script, Dr. Zarniko is described throughout as the Prime Minister. In the English print of the film, the invitation card describes him as Minister of the Interior. In this case, we have followed the script.
** This description in square brackets is taken from the original script. In the National Film Archive print, we follow straight on from the Prime Minister holding the card, to a shot of him bending over his daughter.

makes this wedding impossible!

The girl looks thoughtfully before her, then turns her face to her father and says:

TITLE: *Leave me alone, Daddy. I take no notice at all of these slanders.**

Her father, realising the uselessness of his warnings, resignedly shrugs his shoulders, kisses her forehead and leaves the room. The girl goes on with her typing. Fade to:

Alwa's Room in his Father's House, where Alwa is sitting at the piano, playing. Occasionally he breaks off and writes something in the score-book which lies open on the piano. And at one moment he is so delighted with the tune he has composed that he sings it enthusiastically as he plays.
So he hardly notices when Geschwitz enters, clutching a portfolio under her arm.**
She comes to the piano and smiles as she interrupts his thoughts. He leaps up, delighted to see her, and kisses her hand. Geschwitz lays the big folio on the piano, throws it open and says to Alwa:

TITLE: *I've brought you the costume sketches for your new revue, Alwa.*

Alwa jumps up and the two of them, leaning over the piano, begin to look at the drawings. (Still on page 36)
Geschwitz's hands turn the pages of the sketchbook for Alwa to see. Alwa admires the designs excitedly, lighting cigarettes for them both. As Alwa lights first her cigarette, then his own, Geschwitz stares at him from under the brim of her fashionable, severe hat. It is an intense, meaningful look. She says:

TITLE: *How's Lulu?*

She catches Alwa off his guard. He frowns and avoids her eyes;

---

* In the original script, the Minister's daughter says: 'Don't you think we ought to invite the Heymanns, father?'
** This is Countess Anna Geschwitz. Throughout the original script she is referred to by surname only. Due to the ambivalent relationship between her and Lulu, all scenes with Geschwitz were cut when the film was first released in England.

then he shrugs his shoulders wearily before bringing himself to answer :

TITLE : *Father will have to break with her. The wedding can't be put off any longer.*

Then Lulu comes in. She is elegantly dressed [and nothing about her remains of the little girl who sold flowers in the Alhambra].* She smiles and waves a greeting from the doorway as she bounds in. Camera pans across the room with her as she runs over to where they are standing by the piano. Alwa and Geschwitz both stretch out their hands in delight at seeing Lulu. Holding both their hands, she tells them something. They listen with interest. What is she telling them? Suddenly she lets go of their hands and runs across the room, camera following her, to a curtain rail; and before the two can say anything she has hoisted herself up with one pull and is displaying her newly learned tricks, swinging easily back and forth.

TITLE : *Rodrigo . . . The famous Rodrigo Quast wants to do a Variety act with me. We've already started rehearsing.*

Alwa is watching Lulu, transfixed with delight and amazement at this alluring creature. Geschwitz, by his side, also laughs; but there is a cautious look in her smiling eyes.
Lulu swings happily, backwards and forwards.
Alwa cannot take his eyes off her, while Geschwitz still smiles with interested attention as she watches the half-grotesque, half-charming little scene. Suddenly Alwa dashes forward, leaving Geschwitz watching, a cigarette raised to her lips.
It looks as if the curtain rail might give way. Alwa dashes across and reaches the spot just in time to catch Lulu in his arms as she flings herself, with a bold leap, to the floor. (Still on page 36)
For one moment he has Lulu's face, flushed and laughing, close to his own. She hugs him affectionately and rubs her cheek against his. With a cute little smile she looks into his eyes, then over his shoulder to Geschwitz, and, nodding to her without any embarrassment, says :

TITLE : *Alwa is my best friend — he's the only one who never wants*

---

* Again, this is a reference to Lulu's past life, not shown in the film; see footnote page 18.

29

anything from me . . .

She smiles innocently up at him, her arms still round his neck, holding his face close to hers.

Lulu doesn't notice how stonily Geschwitz stands, her eyes fixed on the couple almost in embarrassment.

For Lulu has already turned back to Alwa and is roguishly threatening him with her index finger under his chin. They chuckle together [as Lulu says:

TITLE: *. . . or is it only because you don't love me that you don't want anything from me?*]

Lulu breaks away and, keeping hold of Alwa's hand, runs back across the room. Alwa follows her every movement with eyes that idolise her.

Still at the piano, Geschwitz has picked up the empty portfolio. As they join her, Lulu pulling Alwa behind her, Geschwitz turns only her head towards them; on her face, usually so well under control, a quick anguished smile.

Lulu notices the drawings laid out on the piano top, and she is electrified by them. She bends over to look more closely, and enthusiastically pulls one of them out.

The costume sketch which so excites Lulu is an extravagant 'gladiator' outfit.

The three of them crowd round the drawing she has picked out as Lulu pleads to Geschwitz:

TITLE: *My dear Countess, you must make me a costume design like that too! [It would look marvellous on the trapeze!]**

Geschwitz agrees and they shake hands on it. But now Geschwitz has to leave and Alwa follows her out, leaving Lulu looking gleefully at the costume sketches.

Alwa has hurried across to see Geschwitz out. At the door, she gives a brief, cold nod to Lulu [and before she goes, she indicates to Alwa that she has left the designs lying on the piano].

Lulu still has the sketch in her hand, and, giving a little leap, she runs with it out of the room into . . .

---

* This reference to Lulu's proposed variety act did not appear on the title card in the National Film Archive print of the film.

Dr. Schön's Large Study, which is empty.
Lulu runs over to the desk where she sees a big photograph. Casually,
she picks it up.
It is a photograph of Dr. Schön's bride-to-be.
Lulu, standing in front of the desk, with good humour and without
jealousy studies the picture. But then Alwa comes in, and she turns
to him at once and asks:

TITLE: *Is she really so beautiful?*

Alwa has no chance to reply because just then Dr. Schön comes in.
He glances at the two, sees the picture in Lulu's hand, goes over to
her in silence, takes the picture from her hand almost brutally and
puts it back firmly in its place. Then he barks at Lulu:

TITLE: *I thought I'd forbidden you to come here!*

Lulu looks up at him in her most haughty way and, putting her
hand on her hip, says, almost aggressively:

TITLE: *I didn't come to see you.*

She meaningfully turns to Alwa and then walks arrogantly away;
Alwa follows. They are about to leave the room when Dr. Schön
calls sharply, explosively:

TITLE: *Alwa!*

Alwa and Lulu look round questioningly.
Dr. Schön considers for a moment; then slowly, wearily, he sits
down.
Lulu stares at him angrily.
Dr. Schön stares back; but not in anger. He stares fixedly, a terrible
burden revealed in his eyes. He says to Alwa:

TITLE: *Please get me down the Encyclopaedia, volume K.*

For a moment Alwa looks at his father in astonishment at this
unusual order; but a smile passes across Lulu's face. She turns to
Alwa, pulls him down by his coat rather closer to her and, to his
great astonishment, kisses him on the mouth. Then she says, as if
incidentally:

TITLE: *As agreed, then, you'll come to see me to-morrow.*

31

As she speaks she smiles sweetly at Alwa. Then, pretending to be indignant, she turns her head, raises her eyebrows and directs a withering glance of contempt at Dr. Schön. Proudly she tosses her head, and with her nose in the air she stalks off.

Dr. Schön stares after her, more than a little disturbed by this display.

Alwa is lost in thought for a moment.

Then he pulls himself together and goes to one of the bookshelves, looks for the required volume, and . . .

Brings it to Dr. Schön, who is still sitting stiffly at his desk. Alwa lays it down beside him, without opening it. For a moment both men are silent. Then Alwa turns away and, without knowing particularly what he is doing, goes to one of the windows. He leans against it and is soon lost in contemplation of the street outside. Meanwhile, Dr. Schön tries to get on with his work. Only he doesn't succeed. He is restless, pushing the things in front of him here and there.

Finally it is his fiancée's picture in front of him, which he pushes aside with an ill-humoured movement. Then he gives up even this attempt at activity, leans back in his chair and sinks into thought.

All at once Alwa breaks the silence by asking softly :

TITLE : *Father, why don't you marry Lulu?*

The horrified Dr. Schön jerks round in his seat. Alwa's question confronts him with a fact that he has repressed in the depths of his unconscious. And he blurts out vehemently :

TITLE : *One does not marry women like that! [It would be suicide.]*

And he jumps up so violently that the heavy chair falls over. He takes no notice of it, for he must master his excitement now by moving.

He begins to walk up and down the room.

Without saying a word, Alwa comes to the desk, picks up the chair, and, taking the costume sketch which Lulu has left lying there, is about to go when . . .

Dr. Schön calls him back, and asks :

TITLE : *What did she want here?*

Alwa shrugs his shoulders, and looks down at . . .

32

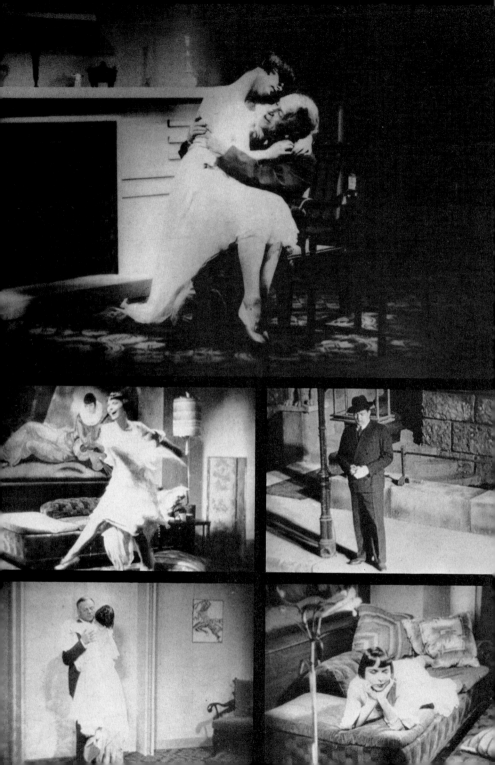

The sketch which he is holding and which captivated Lulu so much. His expression is still quietly melancholic as he looks up from the sketch and back at his father :

Title : *I think she wants to go into Variety. Someone wants to do a trapeze act with her.*

Dr. Schön stares at him for a moment, disconcerted; then, suddenly, he laughs. [He takes a step towards Alwa, claps him on the shoulder. He is shaken by gusts of laughter.]
The sketch which provokes such laughter rests still in Alwa's hand.
Dr. Schön takes it from his son to look at it more closely.
Then, suddenly seized by an idea . . .
He taps Alwa's shoulder with the sketch, and . . .
Taps several times with his finger on the picture.
He smiles at Alwa, pleased with himself.
Alwa looks back, puzzled by this sudden change.
Once again his father taps the drawing. Then he says, dictatorially :

Title : *Not trapeze! She'll play in your revue! She knows how to hop around a bit. And my newspaper guarantees her success!*

Alwa's astonishment changes into enthusiastic agreement. He is carried away by his father's enthusiasm.
Dr. Schön smiles happily back at him. The idea is a good one.
Alwa laughs; he thinks so too.
Dr. Schön laughs out loud in his exuberance.
He takes Alwa by the arm, and together they look again at the costume sketch.
Still pressing the point, and with his hand on his son's arm, Dr. Schön leads Alwa to the door. There are lots of details to arrange, but Dr. Schön is delighted to have hit on such a good way of solving the immediate problem of Lulu's future.
Before they reach the door he stops, turning to Alwa, suddenly serious. Standing over him in a fatherly way, he studies him thoughtfully for a while, affectionately stroking his head.
As he drops his hand to his son's shoulder, he says, so jokingly that the seriousness of the warning isn't at first felt :

Title : *But one thing more, my boy — beware of that girl!*

The effect on Alwa is sudden and dramatic. His smile disappears in a flash. He breaks free from his father, his eyes feverishly casting around for words to say.

Overcome by confusion, he breaks off abruptly and runs out of the room. The door slams behind him. Dr. Schön's cheerful mood suddenly leaves him. He feels the future is full of menace; he stares at the door which he does not dare to open.

Behind the Scenes of a Revue Theatre, the performance is in full swing. The iron pass-door, leading from the auditorium to the stage, is wrenched open and Alwa bursts in. He has Geschwitz with him, looking happy in her evening dress, and carrying a loose bunch of roses in her arms. Alwa is dressed in tails and is visibly excited. As he is beaming, we can assume that his first night is going well. Geschwitz, too, is excited and happy. Alwa shakes hands, vigorously, with the stage doorman.

They push their way through the confused medley of activities which characterise a revue stage — past groups of stage-hands and big pieces of scenery, past dressers, dancing-masters, waiting chorus girls, electricians with spotlights, [past the Director who greets Alwa with a cheerful nod, past the Stage Manager who in spite of his ceaseless activity still finds time to stroke a bare shoulder, or now to clear a way for Alwa]* and then come up to the wings.

Through the narrow opening, Alwa and Geschwitz can see Lulu dancing on stage.

Lulu is wearing the ' gladiator ' costume made up from the design she admired so much out of Geschwitz's collection. She dances confidently on stage, face to face with the invisible public, and then dances out of Alwa's field of vision.

Crowded in the wing, Alwa points her movements out excitedly to Geschwitz.

In Lulu's place on stage come a row of sixteen dancing girls, marching forward in time, and carrying wooden spears.

[Alwa turns round and goes back to where Lulu should come off-stage.]

In the wings, the back-stage activity goes on. A dressing-table has been improvised on a chair, with a looking-glass and make-up box. Beside it, a dresser stands waiting for Lulu's exit, different toilet

---

* In the film, neither the Director nor the Stage Manager appears at this point.

42

articles all ready in her hand. At that moment, a second dresser and a make-up assistant dash up, for Lulu is just dancing from the stage into the wings, right into the excited arms of Alwa and Geschwitz. But before they have had time to greet her properly, the two dressers and the make-up man fling themselves upon their star and begin to get her ready for her next entrance; that is to say, the dressers put new ornaments on her costume while the man freshens up her make-up. Geschwitz hands the besieged Lulu the bunch of roses and embraces her as best she can, for the Stage Manager is already dashing up and telling them to hurry for the next entrance. (Still on page 37) Lulu is radiant. She just finds time to stretch her hand out to Alwa over the wall of people, and he just manages to kiss the tips of her fingers, before she is dragged away by the Stage Manager to the edge of the wings. He snatches the roses from her arm and holds her taut and tense as he listens for her cue. (Still on page 37) When it comes, he pushes her on scene [not forgetting a hasty kiss on the shoulder]. Alwa and Geschwitz crowd round, peering over his shoulder.

On Stage there is a different setting now, since the change of scene; a few dancing girls pose rhythmically in the background. Lulu comes on, dancing, and camera follows her as she flaunts herself across the stage.*

The three look on proudly from the wings at their little star. The Stage Manager blows her kisses, then hastily dashes off to the next emergency.

In the opposite wing, Rodrigo is waiting for his cue. He is also wearing a gladiator's costume and ill-temperedly watches the stage, from which Lulu is just dancing towards him. He nods admiringly, in spite of himself. Lulu stops in front of him, still in her dance costume,** already thinking about her next entrance. Rodrigo snatches the moment to whisper to her:

TITLE : *A lot of rubbish! You'd have done better to do the trapeze*

---

* It is interesting to note, here, that when Lulu receives her cue to go on stage she is still wearing the 'gladiator' costume, with the helmet, etc. In this shot, which supposedly follows without a break for a costume change, she arrives on stage wearing a totally different costume. She has an extravagantly plumed top-piece upon her head and wears a dress with a low-cut bodice.
** Lulu now makes her reappearance in the opposite wing wearing her original 'gladiator' costume.

act with me!

But now the ubiquitous Stage Manager dashes up and all conversation is cut short. He is still carrying the bunch of roses and, although they are obviously in his way, he is too busy even to think about laying them aside. He is following the action in his prompt copy. On cue, he gives the signal to Lulu to go on stage, and at the same time urgently helps Rodrigo on with his helmet and shield. Lulu goes on again, dancing elegantly, and Rodrigo lumbers after her. And behind him appears a second gladiator, then a third, a fourth, then more and more, one after the other, all looking alike, all moving alike — a lumbering chorus. As each one passes the Stage Manager he slams their visors down over their faces, giving the final gladiator a hefty push onto the stage for good measure.

In the throng back-stage, he meets the Director who is just coming down the stairs. Some of the cast are at an opening between the wings, [watching the performance with interest and accompanying it with expressions which show that it is going well].* The Director halts by the Stage Manager and asks him something, pulling out his watch and pointing to it. The Stage Manager's breathlessness increases still further. He also has something urgent on his mind which he must discuss with the Director. He pulls his script out from the bulging pocket of his overall, but in his harassed state he cannot manage both book, flowers, and finger to point with. Feverishly, he passes the flowers over to the Director. They discuss the scene briefly, then the Stage Manager hurries back onto the set.

As he dashes here and there organising the stage-hands with the new scene, he notices that Dr. Schön and his fiancée have just come in through the pass-door. He runs past them with a deep bow.**

In the throng back-stage, the Director is now talking with Alwa.

Dr. Schön and his fiancée come forward behind the scenes, looking up with interest at the staircase, where . . .

We see the chorus girls and actors running quickly down for the next scene.

[While Dr. Schön is still at a distance, the Director is already greeting him effusively; then he claps Alwa on the shoulder and runs over to the couple.]

---

* In the film itself, it is clear that the change of scene mentioned later is already under way.
** End of reel 1.

The Director welcomes Dr. Schön and is himself introduced to the eminent man's fiancée. He conceals his surprise behind exaggerated politeness and, noticing the bunch of roses in his hand, gives a deep bow and presents them to her. Alwa joins them. Radiantly, the girl offers Alwa her congratulations, stretching out her hand to him. But before he can kiss it, the little group is torn apart by the hurtling body of the Stage Manager; when they recover their breath, he points, and they see that he has pushed them all to safety, out of the path of a huge piece of scenery which two scene-shifters are moving across. There is a general sigh of relief and then laughter at the unexpected excitements here, back-stage. Another piece of scenery is moved across the stage.

Dr. Schön and his fiancée have found themselves back-stage at the height of the big scene change which is going on while the performance continues out in front. They are pushed this way and that, under constantly changing directions from the Stage Manager, whenever a scene-shifter has manoeuvred them into a dangerous corner. The girl is neither frightened nor upset, but laughs at this strange and lively chaos. She laughs at . . .

The group of gladiators who leave the stage, marching majestically in time, each carrying in his arms two girls, whom, the moment they are off-stage, they let slide indifferently to the floor.

Dr. Schön laughs gaily with her as . . .

More gladiators come from the stage; the last one is carrying, not a girl on each arm, but a huge fellow gladiator. He drops him to the floor with some relief.

The girl is so absorbed in this sight that she is only just saved from falling into an open trap on the stage by the Stage Manager, who has come dashing up for at least the tenth time. In his zeal to save her, he himself steps backwards onto the trap cover which has reached the floor complete with trees and flower arrangements which the stage-hands have just carried off for the new scene. As the Stage Manager rises on the now re-ascending trap cover, camera tilts up to show him frantically trying to get off.

All the dancing girls pass below him, looking up and laughing at his predicament.

He calls down to them in dismay; it isn't funny, this is serious!

Even Dr. Schön and his fiancée smile as they look up at this strange and amusing sight. Now that they know there is no danger they feel free to enjoy this joke at the Stage Manager's expense.

Meanwhile the poor victim is becoming more and more desperate, frantically looking up, then down for help. Nobody seems to care, nobody appreciates the calamity; everybody seems to think it is funny that he is suspended several feet above the stage right in the middle of a crucial scene-change!

Down below, the gladiators pass and wave cheerily up to him. And the fat ' sheik ' stops to look up, and holds his sides with laughter.

The Stage Manager has had enough. He can't wait for the trap to reach the floor again. But he hesitates; it's a long way down. He banishes fear from his mind, puts his script between his teeth, and, with one upward leap, springs from the trap cover . . .

And lands right on the fat ' sheik's ' broad shoulders. He helps himself to the ' sheik's ' glass of beer and takes a long, needed gulp, before he is carried off, borne easily by the fat man. They go off, followed by other actors; the Stage Manager chaired aloft as though he were leading an Arabian procession.

[Dr. Schön and his fiancée are pushed along by the tide of people. They go towards a quickly erected stair-shaped rostrum up which the Stage Manager is now driving a group of scantily clothed girls. Through the swarm of girls, on whom he doesn't waste a glance,] a little old man comes up — a dresser, who carefully lays out pieces of costume on a chair. An actor dashes across and begins to change his costume, with the old man's help.

Dr. Schön and his fiancée absently watch this scene until the Stage Manager flits across, sizes up the situation, and attracts the girl's attention away from the man undressing in the corner.

The actor, now in his underwear, quite unconcernedly puts on his bow-tie.

The Stage Manager distracts the girl's attention again, and, while her back is turned, urgently tries to make the actor realise the indecency of the situation. Very pointedly, the Stage Manager covers the lower part of his own body with his overall.

But the actor can't understand what's wrong and gestures, pointing to himself in surprise : ' What, me? ' He looks down at himself, closes his legs rather sharply, and the old dresser helps him quickly into his trousers.

The Stage Manager apologises to Dr. Schön, who merely grins. The Stage Manager goes off to deal with further catastrophes.

Back-stage, amid the flurry of activity, he is trying to get things organised; actors and actresses stream past, and huge pieces of scenery are raised for the next act.

Two scene-shifters, moving a gigantic piece of scenery, cut the girl completely off from the scene, and from Dr. Schön. Suddenly she is standing all alone before a huge wall. [She gropes her way to one side of it and then stops.]

Lulu is being undressed. She is changing into a new costume.

As the heavy piece of scenery is taken past her, the girl turns round and stops; for there, before her, she sees Lulu.

Lulu takes no notice either of the girl or of the other people hurrying by, despite the fact that she is half-naked.

By now Dr. Schön is a little anxious about his fiancée. Catching sight of her at last, he comes up, laughing, not noticing Lulu. The Stage Manager rushes past them in his usual frenzy, making them both laugh.

[And Lulu doesn't at first see Dr. Schön either, for one of the dressers has just drawn her skirt over her head. But at the moment when Lulu's head appears out of the folds of clothing, Dr. Schön happens to be looking straight at her. His laugh dies in his throat. For a second, his embarrassment is such that he doesn't know what to do — all the more so, as Lulu now sees him and in expectation of his greeting gives him a friendly smile, while the dressing goes on. But Dr. Schön won't acknowledge her. He takes his fiancée by the arm and hastily leads her away.

Lulu stares after him. As yet she doesn't understand what has happened. Slowly the shameful fact bores its way into her consciousness: Dr. Schön doesn't want to know her. She shakes her head, she wants to make herself believe that all this is not true.] Lulu stands there, adjusting her head-dress and staring, transfixed, at Dr. Schön. The make-up assistant, unaware of all this, has taken a big powder-bowl and is about to go over Lulu's arms and back with a powder-puff.

But Lulu pushes his arm away with such a short, sharp movement that his hand with the powder-bowl is flung into the air and the man's face becomes a mask of white powder, through which two infinitely astonished eyes stare at Lulu. And then she tears off the head-dress which has been so painstakingly arranged, and dashes off, leaving the make-up assistant standing bewildered.

As the truth becomes more and more clear to her, she wants to confront Dr. Schön. But it is into the arms of the harassed Stage Manager that she actually falls, and he, with breathless energy, pushes her right back into the hands of the two dressers, so that they can continue the work of getting her ready to go on. Quickly they start to put her head-dress back on.

But a mood of helpless fury has taken hold of Lulu. She tears off the finery, flinging it at the Stage Manager, and pushes her way out, away from the attentions of the dressers. Camera pans with her as she runs away, followed by the Stage Manager, the two dressers and the make-up man. She is overtaken, held fast, and soon finds herself the centre of an excited ring of people who have hurried to the scene. She fights them all off furiously.

All this hustle and bustle back-stage brings the Director running to the scene to find out what the trouble is.

The Stage Manager is imploring Lulu to be calm, and presses the women and the make-up man to get to work on her again. This has altogether the wrong effect on Lulu. She begins to beat around her wildly, and screams with rage into the face of the Director who has come dashing up :

[TITLE : *I'm not going on again!*]

He remonstrates with her :

TITLE : *Stop playing now!*

[And at that, she starts to tear the costume off her body.]*

In an opening in the wings, Dr. Schön is standing behind his fiancée who is interestedly watching a clown act being played in front of a drop-scene. Dr. Schön looks behind him, for the Director has come up to him softly. With excited, mysterious whispering and a warning look at the girl, he fetches Dr. Schön away, saying :

TITLE : *You must bring her to her senses now.*

Alwa comes to meet his father half-way. He, like the Director, is greatly agitated, and joins him in pleading with his father to talk sense into Lulu. Dr. Schön calms them both with a superior gesture. Confident of his power, he walks through the passage which is opened for him by the group surrounding Lulu. He comes up and

---

* We do not actually see Lulu doing this, but when next seen she is minus all the trappings of her costume.

stands in front of her. (Still on page 38)

Lulu, her rage unabated, looks challengingly at him. Meanwhile the curious onlookers crowd round, Rodrigo among them, anxious not to miss anything.

Dr. Schön bends over Lulu and lectures her.

Lulu stares back resentfully as he wags a threatening finger at her.

Unshaken by her resentment, he goes on lecturing her.

But Lulu will not take this quietly; by now in an absolute fury, she screams back at him.

The Stage Manager looks on, nervously biting his finger-nails, as Dr. Schön *insists* she goes back on stage.

When he actually points to the stage in a commanding gesture, Lulu becomes coolly defiant. She turns her back to him, and sees . . .

Rodrigo, who had been standing behind her; she takes hold of him and says provocatively:

Title: *We'll do our Variety act after all!*

And she pushes off with Rodrigo through the crowd.

Dr. Schön loses his self-control. He thrusts aside the people standing next to him and dashes after Lulu and Rodrigo. Meanwhile the Director comes up to the Stage Manager, looking distinctly concerned.

Rodrigo, delighted, stops with Lulu in a corner back-stage. Dr. Schön comes up to them, whereupon Rodrigo, in his rôle of gallant, steps forward to protect Lulu. But Dr. Schön's rage has been raised to fever pitch by Lulu's resistance, so shaming for him, and he looks at Rodrigo menacingly. And Lulu's gallant defender wants nothing more now than to wriggle out of his rôle as soon as possible. With a feeble show of contempt, he removes himself from the scene. Dr. Schön stands before Lulu. He represses his desire to shout at her, but seizes her violently by the arm.

He tries to drag her off. Lulu slips out of his painful grip, stamping her feet up and down like an uncontrollable child in a temper. Dr. Schön sweeps his arm commandingly towards the stage. [She hisses at him:

Title: *I'll dance for the whole world — but not in front of that woman!*

The girl is still standing in the wings. The trio of clowns on stage are taking several bows as they leave. Just as they are squeezing past the girl, she turns and notices with astonishment that Dr. Schön is not there.]

On stage, where the next scene has been set while all this has been going on, the Stage Manager has got the girls and the performers into their places. (Still on page 38) Seeing that the dance trio has ended, he turns to the wings and nods desperately. At his nod the Director sweeps onto the set, holding out his watch to show the Stage Manager the one fact he already knows only too well : it's time to raise the curtain on the next act. But what can the Stage Manager do if Lulu won't go on? He flings his script to the floor in bitter frustration.

In the corner, Dr. Schön is angrily arguing with Lulu and nodding over at the stage : she *must* go on ! But she won't ! She pulls away from him while he tries to take her forcibly by the arm.

The Stage Manager is still protesting to the Director. Melodramatically, they turn their backs on each other and storm off in opposite directions. The Director runs over to . . .

The corner where Dr. Schön has, for the moment at least, pacified Lulu. He has his arm around her shoulder and is leading her to the quiet of the property room where they can talk in peace. As they reach the door, the Director comes up, breathlessly, and catches hold of him, [pointing despairingly to the stage]. Dr. Schön turns and says to him, over his shoulder :

TITLE : *It's all right, tell them to start!*

The Director sighs with relief as the door is slammed in his face. He claps his hands and gives the Stage Manager an affirmative nod.

The Stage Manager comes flying onto the stage and gives the sign to the curtain operator and electricians. [The spotlights blaze up.] The curtain operator begins to pull up the heavy curtain.

[At the last moment the Stage Manager slips from the scene, and the girls dance row by row down the steps.

Outside the Property Room, the Stage Manager comes running up looking for Lulu. A stage-hand, grinning, points his thumb at the property room door. The Stage Manager dashes towards it.

In the middle of all the senseless and dust-covered junk in the property room, Dr. Schön confronts Lulu. (Still on page 39) All his restraints have fallen away from him and he is shouting at her with

50

distorted features.

But, just as before, she goes on shaking her head in automatic rejection.]*

Suddenly the Stage Manager comes bursting into the room. He stops in the doorway, putting his hand to his mouth in surprise at the sight of . . .

Dr. Schön holding Lulu closely in his arms. Dr. Schön turns round, furious at this intrusion.

There in the doorway he sees the despairing figure of the Stage Manager, his hands folded in supplication.

Dr. Schön lets go of Lulu's arms and springs across and throws him out, shutting the door angrily in the man's face. The Stage Manager gestures wildly, and in his anxiety gets his arm caught in the door. He wiggles his hand around ridiculously.

Outside the Property Room, the Stage Manager is desperately trying to pull his hand free from the door. At last he manages it, and, freed from his support, he falls against the brick wall, giving his head a sharp crack. All his breathless energy immediately evaporates. He rubs his head and his hand. The catastrophe, unforeseen and not fitting into his script, has thrown him right off his course. Perplexed and helpless, he stands with shaking knees outside the closed door, wiping the sweat from his forehead with a dirty white handkerchief. [For the first time, he turns to his script for help, leafing through the pages with trembling hands.]

In the Property Room, Dr. Schön's struggle with Lulu has reached a climax. He is foaming with rage; it looks as if he is going to hit her. Lulu's temper, too, is verging on hysteria. She is incapable of answering him. With her bare back turned towards him, she covers her ears with her hands. [With two or three mad, sharp pulls, she tears off her dress.] She continues to shake her head — she *won't* go on!

Dr. Schön's rage is uncontrollable. He shakes her furiously.

Lulu resists convulsively, hysterically. She leans against the shelves which are filled with the thousand dead things waiting for the stage lighting to bring them to life. Her head falls back and soundlessly, unsteadily, she begins to weep, still shaking her head obstinately

---

* This description in square brackets is taken from the original script, and was not seen in the version screened.

from side to side.

[And now Dr. Schön feels himself at the end of his tether. Weakly he confronts the woman he loves. His brutal domineering attitude collapses, his confident movements become unsettled, his angrily clenched hands open, then close again. He stands pleading, even begging, before Lulu. In Lulu, too, a change is taking place.]

Outside the Property Room, the Stage Manager, who is still wiping his face with the handkerchief, gives a philosophical shrug. He's not going to worry any more. Let them get on with it — he doesn't care!

On stage, between two big wings, we see that the performance is already in progress. In the foreground stand Alwa and the Director. Instead of the usual excitement there is an oppressed silence.

One of the actors plays himself towards the wings, frowning an urgent message at the Director:

TITLE : *Where's Lulu?*

The Director spreads his arms, as if to say : ' What can I do ? ' And Alwa does the same. The Director turns round and runs off. Alwa is about to follow him, when his father's fiancée appears, bewildered, and asks him a question. Alwa, visibly embarrassed, avoids answering her.

In the Property Room, Dr. Schön has a cigarette in his mouth. With angry movements he is trying to light a match, but in his temper all he does is break it.

Lulu has thrown herself, face down, onto a pile of cushions and costumes, and is sobbing convulsively. For a moment she raises her tear-stained face to see what Dr. Schön is doing.

But then she quickly goes on sobbing even more; punching the costumes beneath her in hysterical anger, trying to attract his attention. Dr. Schön, his face set and his back to Lulu, puts the cigarette back in his down-turned mouth, and hunts in his pockets for another match.

Unexpectedly, Lulu's feet kick him sharply around the ankles. Between sobs she says:

TITLE : *Smoking's not allowed in here.*

Dr. Schön, the lighted match in his raised hand, turns with upraised eyebrows at this incongruous remark. He looks blankly at Lulu . . .

52

Who has gone back to her agonised sobbing.

In a sudden rage, he flings both match and cigarette to the floor.

Stuffing his hands in his pockets, he begins to stalk around the room. He walks up and down, then from side to side, then up and down again, glancing helplessly at Lulu's pathetic form, stretched out as it is, face down on the pile of costumes. She is sobbing and kicking her feet in frustration. Lulu's weeping has a remarkable effect on Dr. Schön. From having wanted to hit her a little while ago, he now kneels down beside her. Bending over her tossing head, his hands reach out to dry her eyes with his handkerchief. [He takes her by the shoulders and gently, caressingly, strokes Lulu's arms. His head sinks towards her, sinks down to her, leans against her shoulder. And the tall, once angry man caresses Lulu's body from head to foot. Lulu's face becomes calmer, brightens. Motionless, she lets his caresses play over her, while her eyes close with pleasure.]

At last she is in his arms in a tight embrace; helplessly he has surrendered to her, his arm round her shoulder, his fingers running through her hair.

The door is suddenly pushed open. Alwa stares in horror into the room. And behind him stands Dr. Schön's fiancée. She stares, gazes with wide-open eyes at the spectacle.

Dr. Schön is lying back on the pile of costumes with the half-naked Lulu wrapped in his arms, covering him with kisses. Lulu looks up at the sound; but he hears nothing, so absorbed is he in Lulu. (Still on page 40)

Alwa cannot move; he stares, frozen in horror. The girl has a stony, dignified expression on her face. [Alwa tries quickly to shut the door, but the girl prevents him by stretching out her arm in a commanding gesture.

Lulu's eyes stare at this little scene. Dr. Schön suddenly awakens from his absorption, turns around and looks up at . . .

The doorway where his fiancée is standing with her eyes fixed on him, lying there in Lulu's arms. But just then, she is pushed aside by the Stage Manager, breathless once more, now that the calamity can be averted. With clasped hands, he implores Lulu to come with him. Lulu has won. Victoriously she gathers up her costume. Without a look at Dr. Schön, she dashes off through the door with the Stage Manager.]

We see the Stage Manager come leaping triumphantly from the

room, past Alwa and Dr. Schön's fiancée in the doorway, pulling the jubilant Lulu behind him. Camera pans across with them as Lulu runs into the hands of the make-up man and the wardrobe mistress, who rush to get her ready once more. Someone hands her the head-dress; another re-laces her costume. All is a bustle of activity again. The Stage Manager wipes his face with relief. Lulu is as happy as a child.

Still in the doorway, the girl stares fixedly at this scene. She half turns and stands for a while with a sunken head. Then, without raising her head, she turns about and walks silently and slowly towards the pass-door.

Just as she is about to open it, Alwa, who has followed her, comes up and looks at her imploringly, holding the door closed. But the girl only looks at him with big, despondent eyes. She then shakes her head gently, so that Alwa gives way and lets her open the door. She goes out. He stands gloomily in the open doorway for a moment, looking hopelessly after her.

[Lulu is not yet ready when her cue comes, and the Stage Manager pushes her onto the stage. The make-up man, with outstretched hand, is still powdering her back.]

In the open doorway of the Property Room, Dr. Schön appears. His hair is wild, his tie undone. Mechanically, he puts his hand to his tie, but brokenly he drops his arm again. All he can do is lean wearily against the brick wall and wipe his face. His eyes stare dumbly at the stage where the radiant Lulu is now dancing. (Still on page 40)

The Stage Manager falls, shaken and exhausted but happy, into the nearest chair. With the calm air of one whose life verges always on the catastrophic, he takes a limp sandwich from his pocket and begins to eat. But no, it's not over yet; suddenly seeing or remembering something, he leaps up, abandoning the sandwich for the latest unpredictable calamity.

Dr. Schön is still leaning against the wall, wiping his face with his handkerchief, when Alwa comes up. The two men look at one another. Dr. Schön has given way to despair :

TITLE : *Are you satisfied, Alwa? I'll marry Lulu. That'll be the end of me.*

And he stares up with glassy eyes as he finishes speaking these

54

dreadful words, the handkerchief pressed to his lips. Alwa sinks his head. Dr. Schön lays his hand, as if looking for support, on Alwa's shoulder, and while his eyes are fixed on the stage, he murmurs, more to himself than to his son :

TITLE : *That is my execution.*

We are in Dr. Schön's Large Study. It has been cleared and turned into a reception room. Only the bookshelves and pictures are a reminder of former seriousness. The room is separated only by a balustrade from the window gallery which connects Alwa's room with Dr. Schön's bedroom. The room itself is somewhat higher, and some stairs lead down to the gallery. Groups of women in full evening dress and men in tails are standing around. In the middle of the room, couples are dancing. Through an open door we can see into another room, where evidently a buffet has been set up. Waiters, in tails with metal buttons, are serving champagne and liqueurs. The revelry seems to be at its height. Dr. Schön is standing at the head of the stairs, receiving his guests. In the button of his tailcoat, he is wearing a sprig of myrtle blossom. He is surrounded by two or three men, and greeting two guests who have just arrived and are offering him their congratulations.
He kisses the hand of one of them — a well-dressed lady.
Still holding her hand, he shakes that of her escort and glances searchingly round the room.
The guests are seen dancing happily in the middle of the room.
Dr. Schön's expression darkens for a moment, but he turns back at once to his guests with an uncertain smile.
Two Americans come through the dancing throng to greet him.
They come up and shake his hand. Smiling their congratulations, Dr. Schön exchanges pleasantries with them.
We find ourselves in a sort of broad corridor in the service rooms in Dr. Schön's house. At one end, stairs lead up to the living-rooms, while at the other an open door shows a room which evidently serves as a pantry. This room is the focus of the most vigorous movement, as there is an uninterrupted flow of waiters, and often of uniformed waitresses, hurrying to and from the stairs.
Lulu comes down these stairs, past the waiters, who admiringly make way for her. She is in full bridal costume, carrying her train over

55

her arm and in a radiant mood. We follow her along the corridor as far as the curtained entrance, round which she peeps mischievously. She laughs excitedly as she comes through, and camera follows her until she stops by a small table in the corner where Schigolch and Rodrigo are sitting. They, too, are in tails. But while Schigolch seems to have shrunk into the folds of his suit, Rodrigo fills his out so much that it is almost bursting at the seams. Their mood is more than merry. When Lulu laughingly asks how they are doing, Rodrigo regretfully produces an empty champagne bottle. Lulu lifts it up and shakes it.

The chef, who has just helped himself to a drink, looks up from his work and smirks at the delightful little bride.

Lulu won't have her special guests going without drinks. She turns round on the spot and takes a bottle of champagne from one of the waiters hurrying past, [and from another a bottle of liqueur]. A maid comes out of the pantry, carrying a dish of fine confectionery which Lulu takes from her and lays before Schigolch and Rodrigo, both of whom immediately set to. Not content, Lulu dashes off for more.

The chef, who is just finishing his liqueur, still has his eyes appraisingly fixed on Lulu. A maid, working beside him, strains her neck to see this strange pair, who are kept apart from the other guests, yet treated so lavishly by Dr. Schön's new bride.

Lulu comes back to the table triumphantly bearing a huge tray of delicacies for Rodrigo and Schigolch. They beam in drunken pleasure. Laughing, Lulu pushes Rodrigo back in his seat. Schigolch offers her his liqueur glass and Lulu takes a sip from it. As she hands it back, he takes hold of her wrist to draw her down towards him, but with an affectionate smile she breaks away and runs back up the stairs. Schigolch leans back, his eyes half-closed, glass raised to his lips, his other arm outstretched as though it was still holding Lulu.

In Dr. Schön's Large Study, Alwa is leaning by the door leading into the room where the buffet has been laid. Lulu appears in the doorway. She sees him and saucily invites him to dance with her.

Geschwitz is standing alone on the other side of the room, near a group of unpartnered females. She is staring at Alwa and Lulu.

Alwa, with an obvious effort to hide his anguish, refuses Lulu's invitation. Lulu turns away and notices . . .

56

Geschwitz, who clearly isn't going to let Lulu out of her sight.

Lulu smiles and hurries over to her . . .

She takes Geschwitz by the arm and begins dancing with her. Before the pair vanish among the crowd of other dancers, we see Geschwitz's face transfigured with joy. She holds Lulu close to her as she dances.

Alwa's eyes are dark and brooding as he watches the two women dancing closely together.

Geschwitz leads Lulu round the dance floor. Lulu's eyes are now on Alwa.

At the balustrade, Dr. Schön is still standing with the Americans. His eyes, restlessly searching the room, at last notice . . .

Lulu and Geschwitz as they dance by. Geschwitz has her eyes closed and her cheek pressed close against Lulu's. As they circle round, Lulu's face can be seen over Geschwitz's shoulder. She is smiling happily. She catches sight of her new husband and sees . . .

That he is staring at her.

She smiles.

He looks at them, also smiling, but with narrowed eyes.

Geschwitz, unaware of Dr. Schön, goes on leading Lulu round and round. If she does notice that Dr. Schön is watching them with such restrained agitation, her face shows no evidence of it; she dances on, her expression set.

Dr. Schön asks the Americans to stay where they are for a moment, and heads for the dancing couple.

With a quick stride he steps up to the pair and politely bows. Absorbed in their dance, they are not at first aware of his presence. Lulu looks up (Still on page 73) and as they break apart, Dr. Schön invites Lulu to come and meet the two Americans. Then he turns, with Lulu on his arm.

He brings her towards the Americans and introduces them to his young wife. She shakes hands demurely. The Americans, visibly enchanted by her, congratulate him.

Geschwitz is now standing on the outside of the circle of dancers, a brooding intensity disfiguring her features. A young man approaches her and invites her to dance. She starts out of her daydream, declines with confusion but quite firmly, then walks morosely away.

By Dr. Schön's group a waiter stands with the champagne. The Americans are drinking a toast with Lulu and Dr. Schön, who

57

solemnly toast each other.

Some waiters and two or three maids are standing around Schigolch and Rodrigo at their corner table in the service rooms. They are listening with laughter to Rodrigo's big talk, while Schigolch, crying drunk, pours out champagne for them.

A maid comes down the stairs carrying some roses. She joins the group and is at once seized by Rodrigo, who takes her on his knee and tries roughly to kiss her. When she tries to protect herself with the roses, he snatches them from her hand and throws them onto the table. Schigolch picks up the flowers and stares at them thoughtfully.

Laughing hysterically, the maid makes a show of resisting Rodrigo's drunken embraces.

Something like a touch of sentiment penetrates Schigolch's alcohol-sodden brain as he gazes at the flowers in his arms. A maudlin grin spreads over his face and, in a voice almost choked with tears, he says:

TITLE: *A regular low-down cur I should be if I didn't lay a rose on my little Lulu's bridal bed.*

The group around the table receive this remark with a screech of laughter. Schigolch is lifted up and pushed towards the stairs. But since he is hardly capable of standing upright by himself and is only fit for dreamily blowing kisses into the air, Rodrigo gets up too, and takes him by the arm. The two of them are pushed out by the laughing servants.

Together, they totter up the stairs, grabbing bottles and more flowers on the way, amid the cheers of the servants who stay behind.

The servants all laugh merrily at the pair.

Rodrigo picks more flowers from the pots on the staircase to add to Schigolch's bunch.

The servants start to drift away; they have work to get on with in the pantry.

We are in the corridor at the top of the stairs. The first door leads into the room where the buffet is laid, while the last door, at the end of the corridor, leads into Dr. Schön's bedroom. [Schigolch and Rodrigo come stumbling up the stairs. Schigolch, with the obstinacy of a drunken man, is now dragging Rodrigo after him. Rodrigo, half laughing and half in anger, is trying to prevent the old man carrying out his idea.] On tables, even on chairs, there are masses of flowers arranged in vases. Probably they have been sent to the young bride. Schigolch stands quietly looking at these flowers, and makes his choice as if in a flower shop, treating Rodrigo as if he were the shopkeeper. [Two of the serving men come up the stairs, nudge one another with giggles at the sight of Schigolch, then earnestly and solemnly enter the reception rooms.]

Rodrigo gallantly picks flower after flower for Schigolch, who already has his arms packed full. Two guests appear in the corridor, refreshing themselves after dancing with a smoke and a chat. Rodrigo makes Schigolch aware of the guests by nudging the drunken fellow into following his own example of bowing respectfully. Schigolch does so. Then Rodrigo puts a supporting arm round Schigolch's shoulder, and together they go off. The guests stand watching this strange show and snigger to themselves as the pair pass, with their heads held high, going towards the far end of the corridor.

Back in the reception room, Lulu and Dr. Schön are standing by the balustrade. Lulu is hanging on her husband's arm. She draws him with an affectionate whisper down the stairs towards the bedroom door which is seen in the background. But they are hardly two stairs down, when Dr. Schön has to turn back. Their intended flight has been noticed, and some friends of the house are grouping themselves up at the balustrade with laughing, joyful comments. Dr. Schön releases himself from Lulu and goes back up to the guests.

Meanwhile, Lulu flits on down the stairs. Camera pans with her until she reaches the bedroom door.

With outspread arms, Dr. Schön holds back the guests, who are trying to take their leave of him.

He nods smilingly; they must not dream of leaving yet. The band is to keep on playing. Obediently, the musicians take up their instruments again.

Dr. Schön waves gaily at the band to begin the music. A man and a woman, standing on the dance floor, begin to dance again.

Dr. Schön smiles warmly at his guests.

Lulu, standing by the bedroom door, looks back at her husband. He turns.

She signals to him flirtatiously, with a little nod that he should join her.

59

Dr. Schön returns the signal with another affectionate nod; but he must first turn to some more of the guests.

He turns round to his guests once again, smiling warmly.

A group of waiters and maids have just entered the reception room, carrying silver platters with sausages and beer for the guests.

Dr. Schön now draws his guests' attention to this new arrival. With a cheer, the guests surround the serving men.

Lulu is just about to enter the bedroom, when Geschwitz suddenly appears beside her. She looks solemnly at Lulu for a moment, then sharply and violently clutches her tightly, and just as quickly disappears. Lulu laughs and enters the bedroom.

Lulu comes into the bedroom, shuts the door behind her, and starts to take off her bridal veil. She turns round and stares in surprise at something in the room, then bursts out laughing.

Beside the wide bed Schigolch is standing and, with priestly gestures, is strewing his flowers over the pillows and coverlet. Rodrigo stands limply beside him.

The flowers are heaped in glorious profusion all over the bed.

Lulu is delighted.

Schigolch is so absorbed in his efforts that he has not even noticed her. He goes on throwing the flowers with delighted abandon.

Lulu runs up to him.

Impetuously, she embraces the old man, overwhelmed by his devotion.

Rodrigo is now pouring some champagne into an ashtray from the bottle he has brought with him.

Schigolch, with tottering solemnity, draws Lulu's head down to him and kisses her forehead.

Having managed to pour the champagne without spilling too much, Rodrigo drinks to Lulu's health from it.

Alwa is leaning against the wall by the window gallery which is between the balustrade and the bedroom. He is brooding, absorbed in his thoughts.

Dr. Schön is standing at the balustrade, also deep in thought. He comes down the stairs . . .

And goes as far as the bedroom door, when he stops short.

Alwa sees his father and calls out to him. Hastily, he puts out his cigarette on the table behind him, and comes anxiously towards his father.

[Dr. Schön lays his hand on Alwa's arm. Alwa turns his face towards his father and with a strained laugh tries to hide his feelings. The father strokes his son's arm soothingly, and also gently strokes his hair. Then he claps him roughly once or twice on the shoulder to hide his own emotion, and goes to move on. Alwa holds him back.] Dr. Schön looks questioningly at Alwa, who after a short pause says:

TITLE: *Father . . . I am going away tonight . . . for a long time . . .*

Dr. Schön looks at his son in surprise, then gives a brief nod. [He holds out his hand to Alwa. Both men shake hands.] They look at each other silently for a while, until Alwa turns slowly and leaves. His father follows him sadly with his eyes.

In Dr. Schön's Bedroom, Lulu is pulling at Schigolch's arm, trying to get the two uninvited guests out of the room — but her attempts are defeated by Schigolch's drunkenness. He is no longer capable of judging the situation and falls down giggling onto the edge of the bed. As Lulu tries to get him to his feet and drag him away, he pulls her down onto his lap. Indulgently, she kisses him, trying at the same time to get him up.

At this moment Dr. Schön comes in. He is smiling with genial anticipation as his eyes search out Lulu. Then his expression changes; he has seen Rodrigo.

Rodrigo is gleefully pouring out more champagne and laughing at the pair on the bed.

Dr. Schön follows Rodrigo's gaze. Already his face is creased with horrified bewilderment at the sight of this drunken fellow in his bedroom. But now he sees . . .

Lulu, who is trying to break free from Schigolch's grasp. The old man kisses her hand and Lulu responds with an affectionate smile.

Dr. Schön remains standing in the doorway. He wears the expression of a man who has received a violent blow on the head. He wants to shout, but his mouth opens without a sound being uttered. He takes out his monocle and stares back at Rodrigo.

Rodrigo is just lifting the champagne-filled ashtray to his lips again. Suddenly his chuckle freezes in his throat — he has caught sight of Dr. Schön standing in the open doorway.

Dr. Schön seems, for a moment, to recover his senses. He closes the door firmly behind him.

But his appearance is still so frightening that Rodrigo's primitive instinct impels him to be conciliatory. Awkwardly, in his outstretched hand and keeping himself as far away as possible, he offers Dr. Schön the glass ashtray filled with champagne.

Dr. Schön has the expressionless face of a man who has lost his senses. His mouth has fallen dumbly open. He drags himself across the room to where . . .

Rodrigo is still pathetically holding the glass ashtray out to him. Dr. Schön stops right in front of him. (Still on page 73)

Suddenly Lulu, in the midst of her playful fight with Schigolch, looks up, and for the first time sees Dr. Schön standing so ominously over Rodrigo.

Rodrigo is still foolishly holding the drink out to Dr. Schön.

Panic-stricken, Lulu is fighting the old man in deadly earnest now, trying to free herself from his embrace. Until this moment, she has not been able to jolt Schigolch into realising how dangerous the situation is.

But she is too late to prevent Dr. Schön from waking out of his stunned paralysis and knocking the glass ashtray out of Rodrigo's hand. Rodrigo, coward as he is, tries to defend himself with the champagne bottle. But before he can strike Dr. Schön, Lulu breaks free from the drunken Schigolch's clasp and bursts into Rodrigo's arms, throwing him easily off balance. (Still on page 74)

Schigolch, from his position on the bed, looks on in dazed horror at these events. Through champagne-glazed eyes he sees . . .

Lulu hanging round Rodrigo's neck. He raises the champagne bottle to strike Dr. Schön.

Dr. Schön clearly misinterprets Lulu's action. The sight of his young bride hanging onto Rodrigo sends him mad with rage. He turns away from them, his face suddenly expressionless . . .

And turns farther round, hiding the sight of them from his eyes . . .

With groping hands he reaches towards the drawer of a nearby piece of furniture and snatches it open.

Behind him, Lulu is still frantically hanging onto Rodrigo's neck.

From the drawer, Dr. Schön pulls out a revolver.

This outbreak of Dr. Schön's sets Schigolch in motion. He jumps up like a rat in a trap, his eyes darting restlessly about the room.

Dr. Schön stands holding the revolver, looking murderously from one to the other.

Schigolch raises his hands in terror. He sees that his escape towards the corridor is barred by Dr. Schön, so he flits to the door through which Dr. Schön himself entered.

His flight draws Dr. Schön's attention to him. Dr. Schön turns towards the fleeing man, then Lulu throws herself on his back and, with her arms choking him, screams at him to stop.

Schigolch stands at the door in terror, his hands high above his head. Lulu has Dr. Schön in a vice-like grip, as she cries :

TITLE : *He's my father!*

But with a great heave, Dr. Schön throws Lulu aside, tears himself away from her and runs after the two men.

For Rodrigo is also running now. With his hands above his head, he too has reached the door. Schigolch opens it, and the two terrified figures hurry out, running as fast as they can with their arms stretched right up above them.

In Dr. Schön's Large Study, Schigolch and Rodrigo dash up the stairs and, in their terror, run right into the middle of the guests. The appearance of these two grotesque figures draws the guests' attention.

Schigolch and Rodrigo stand perplexed in the middle of the elegant company. The guests crowd round, staring curiously at them.

Alwa, who has also witnessed the scene, runs down the stairs. At the foot of the stairs his father passes, without noticing him, going in the other direction.

Schigolch and Rodrigo turn and look in Dr. Schön's direction.

He has positioned himself on the edge of the circle of guests. He still has the revolver in his hand.

Seeing Dr. Schön with the revolver, Schigolch jumps with fright and hastily raises his hands again.

Dr. Schön starts to come threateningly forward.

This is enough to put Schigolch and Rodrigo to flight again. The strong man once more puts up his hands, and then the two of them run through a lane opened for them by the guests, and go out by the nearest door. Dr. Schön has come too late. He stands in the middle of the room with the gun raised above his shoulder as the guests spread back in a wide circle around him. There is a deathlike silence over them all. He lets the gun fall to his side.

Dr. Schön can now find no words to explain this incredible episode which has disrupted his wedding reception. He stares around him dumbly.

He seems as if he is not quite in his right mind. When one or two of his friends come closer and try to help him, he only looks vacantly into their faces, as if he does not know them. The guests begin to leave the room; the atmosphere has become quite sinister. They leave in groups, whispering together, glancing round in embarrassment at Dr. Schön. Some of them bow without a word, and bit by bit they all go out.

Alwa is standing in the middle of Dr. Schön's bedroom beside Lulu. He is pleading with her, violently, anxiously. As he does so, he lays a brightly-coloured cloak with a broad fur collar about her shoulders. He lets his arm lie on her shoulder as he presses her in the direction of the door to the corridor. Lulu resists; she doesn't want to run away. Alwa presses her, pointing warningly to the other door through which he is afraid his father will enter at any moment. But Lulu frees herself and sits down in the corner of a big armchair. The cloak falls off her shoulders as she sits. Alwa stands in front of her, and implores her to escape. But she only shakes her head in refusal.

Dr. Schön is still standing in the middle of the large study, which all the guests are rapidly leaving. The gun hangs limply by his side. The musicians, having packed up their instruments, are walking on tiptoe one after another, hugging the walls, out of the room.

Alwa is still arguing with Lulu in the bedroom. He seizes her hand, once more he tries to pull her away. He whispers :

TITLE : *Wouldn't you like to go with me?**

And when Lulu laughingly shakes her head at the idea . . .

Alwa drops his head into her lap and absentmindedly begins to kiss her folded hands. In gasps the words come from his lips :

TITLE : *I can't live without you any longer!*

Back in the large study, Dr. Schön takes in the scene, looking twice round the empty room. Bitterly, he shrugs his shoulders and then goes slowly, wearily towards the balustrade. Here he stops a moment

---

* In the original script, Alwa says: ' If you would only come with me . . . '

and looks thoughtfully down the barrel of the gun. Then he lets it drop to his side once more as he goes down the steps and across to an alcove. Some glasses of beer are standing on the side table. The beer is already flat, but he takes a sip.

In the bedroom Alwa is kneeling at Lulu's feet. He has buried his head in her lap and she soothingly strokes his hair.

Dr. Schön puts the glass back on the table. It seems as if by doing so he has come to terms with his destiny, for he walks back lightly [down the stairs and turns towards the bedroom. After a few steps, he pauses once more. Through the open door he sees inside the room].

Lulu lifts her head and looks up. Her husband is coming towards her. (Still on page 75) She sees, but she does not move; she just goes on looking. Dr. Schön's hand with the gun comes into view, limply resting against his side, as he stops behind the kneeling Alwa. His son has noticed nothing, and still has his head buried in Lulu's lap. Dr. Schön stares down at the scene. (Still on page 75)

Alwa, his eyes closed, still has not looked up.*

Like a man paralysed by his thoughts, Dr. Schön just stares at the two young people.

Lulu looks up at him steadily with her wide eyes. She does not seem afraid.

Her husband stares back at her. His face is heavy with sorrow. Slowly, his eyes pull themselves away from Lulu and drag his vision down to Alwa. Heavily, as if forcing his body to move, he starts to lean forward. He lays his hand on Alwa's shoulder and tries to wake him up. Alwa raises his head and looks up at his father, confusion and horror instantly filling his eyes.

Dr. Schön watches him dumbly as he rises to his feet. Then he leans forward again, and, roughly taking him by the arm, shakes Alwa. He brings his son's face close to his, and for a moment it seems as if his iron self-control must snap, but he only says, looking deep into Alwa's eyes:

TITLE : *You'll . . . miss . . . your . . . train!*

The two men look at one another, without hate . . . without apology . . . Then, like a sleepwalker, Alwa allows his father to lead him off.

---

* End of reel 2.

Lulu has not moved from her chair. She watches the scene silently. At the door, Alwa stares at his father, who is still holding him by the arm. Without altering his gaze, Alwa slowly opens the door and, keeping his eyes on his father as he goes, moves slowly away and disappears. Dr. Schön gazes after his son until he has gone from sight. Then he slams the door shut and bolts it.

Lulu sits staring in front of her.

Dr. Schön makes sure the door is firmly locked.

Lulu at last breaks out of her trance-like state. She stands up and stares for a moment at her husband. She can learn nothing from his face, which seems changed to stone. Made uneasy by this unexpected calm, she draws back towards the bed, then goes and stands in front of the dressing-table.

Catching sight of herself in the looking-glass, she stretches and draws herself out a little. She has already forgotten her terror, She smiles at herself, puts her hands to her neck and loosens the train from her shoulders, and throws it onto a chair.

Dr. Schön at last turns round from the door. When he catches sight of Lulu he cannot believe his eyes.

Lulu stands in front of the mirror admiring herself: slim, white, innocent. [Now her hands reach for the shoulder clasp and she begins to slip off her dress.] She stops suddenly . . .

Dr. Schön is staring in horror at this display.

But Lulu turns back happily to the mirror and takes off the pearl necklace. She runs it caressingly through her fingers before laying it in the jewel case. As she comes back to the mirror, she stops again, for suddenly reflected in the mirror beside her is her husband. It is almost as if Death were standing there. Out of the dark background a death's-head shines lividly. Only by its burning, menacing eyes does she recognise her husband. She turns to him, one shoulder bared. The image in the mirror is holding the revolver out to her. She starts back in sheer terror, turning from the mirror image to look him in the face. She draws away from him in disbelief and horror.

Terrified by his expression, she retreats backwards, her eyes staring at the gun. He follows her, holding the revolver close in front of her. He seems obsessed by a single idea.

Terrified, she shakes her head as he holds the revolver out to her. She pleads desperately with him.

66

But her husband just stares transfixed by his thoughts, and whispers :

TITLE : *Take it!*

With these words, he presses the weapon against her hand.
And when she looks at him with fear in her eyes [he thrusts his face close to hers, and whispers into her ear :

TITLE : *Kill yourself!*

Her face opens wide with horror, her mouth stays open, but she does not scream].
His hand takes hold of her clenched hand and forces her to open it and grip the gun. She tries to shove the gun away, but he grips it, and bends her wrist right round so that the deadly barrel is directed against her bared breast. And with strength that is almost irresistible, he forces his will upon her :

[TITLE : *Kill yourself . . . it's the only way to save us!*]

Lulu is frozen with horror and fear. The gun is pointing right at her face now. Desperately, she pushes it away.
He forces his strength against her, pushing the gun round to point at her body.
The revolver is now pointing up at her face.
For a moment Dr. Schön's face almost softens. Yet, driven by his torment, he says :

TITLE : *You must kill yourself!*

He presses close to her again, bearing down on her with all his weight. The revolver is between them. She seems paralysed by fear as he presses down on her. Then suddenly there is a rage of resistance in Lulu. Dr. Schön's powers of suggestion do not reach her ultimate will to live. Slowly she can force herself to overcome her paralysis, slowly she can turn the menacing barrel away from her. She screams at last :

TITLE : *I won't!*

Yet again the man's fanatical will turns the weapon towards her. He is blinded to all but one thought : he won't be crossed now. They struggle. His broad back, bent over Lulu's tiny form, almost hides her from view. But suddenly the tension dissolves in a terrible cry. Lulu's whole body stiffens and resists. And smoke rises in the space between them as Dr. Schön begins to fall away from Lulu. Lulu watches, wide-eyed, as the great figure sways, first forward, then back, like a mountain about to crush her, then rocks unsteadily away from her.

Possessed by pain and horror, the heavy figure staggers across the room and stops in front of the bed. Unable to force his body to stay upright any longer, he falls and crashes down onto the bed.

Lulu is transfixed; she watches him in terror.

Incredibly, he rises to his feet and, summoning all his will and determination, lurches back across the room to Lulu.

She stands motionless, staring up at him as he approaches. Her face mingles fear and pity, for now he has reached out his hands, and gently has taken her head in them, and, putting his arms protectively round her neck, draws her to him for a final, forgiving kiss. But his head falls to her breast, his hands drop. He slides slowly down her body. (Still on page 76)

And slowly slides to the ground, crouching there.

Suddenly Alwa plunges through the door of the bedroom. His horrified eyes see his father's broad back, apparently bent over something. Dr. Schön, bent in agony, lifts out his hand, beckoning urgently for Alwa to come to him. Alwa flies to his side. Using his son as a support, Dr. Schön tries to rise from the floor. Alwa struggles with the heavy body of his father.

Dr. Schön puts his arm round Alwa's neck, then pulls desperately at Alwa's hair, trying to steady himself. But his head will not stay upright; it lolls drunkenly to one side as his eyes roll upward and a thick line of blood trickles out from the corner of his mouth and runs down his chin. Alwa stares, aghast, as his father vainly tries to speak. (Still on page 77) Holding his father in his arms, Alwa catches the dying man's last look and hears through his death rattle :

[TITLE : *Beware, Alwa! You're the next!*]*

All at once he begins to fall, and Alwa cannot hold the weight of his father's dying body. He pulls him back once, but it is like a lump of lead, and, only just keeping his own balance, Alwa has to let him fall.

---

* In the film, Dr. Schön does try to speak, but this title card did not appear in the version screened.

The body falls to a heap on the floor.
Alwa looks up in horror at Lulu. She is watching, frozen.
Dr. Schön lies between their feet.
Alwa draws back. His mind cannot take all this in. Lulu only stares
with wide-open, expressionless eyes. In her hand is the revolver,
pointed downwards at the dead body of Dr. Schön lying on the
floor at her feet.*

In a Court of Justice.

TITLE : *My Lord, I have given the court a brief description of some
terrible events . . .*

TITLE : *Gentlemen of the Jury! Look at this woman . . .*

The Defending Counsel, who seems to be in a state of considerable
excitement, turns to the jury box :

TITLE : *Have I not proved to you that this woman has committed
no murder . . . that her husband was the unfortunate victim of a
chain of fateful coincidences . . . ?*

The Jurymen turn their attention to the dock where . . .
Lulu is sitting [between two warders] looking steadily in front of
her. She is in deep mourning. She has thrown back the widow's
veil from her face. Camera pans to show the Defending Counsel
just below her as he walks away, continuing his speech. He speaks
with passion, leaning forward from his place; his arm stretched out
oratorically towards the jury box.
He turns and faces the open courtroom :

TITLE : *Did not the dead man's son even speak up on behalf of this
woman?*

Alwa is sitting hunched forward, his eyes cast down. The women in
the public seats behind him crane their necks to see . . . Feeling
himself the centre of all attention, he leans farther forward [and
buries his face in his hands]. Camera starts to pan along the row.
It stops first on Schigolch, who is sitting beside Alwa. He looks at
Alwa sideways, a half smile on his lips as he hears the Counsel's

---

* The original script had at this point the following description :
'Lulu stands with wide-open expressionless eyes. In her hand the revolver,
pointed upwards, still goes on firing shot after shot.'

69

words. Camera pans as he turns his head and makes a remark to Rodrigo, who is sitting on the other side of him. Rodrigo nods with a grin. Camera moves on to reveal Geschwitz sitting next to Rodrigo, who leans sideways and whispers to her. She merely gives a brief, off-hand nod, and, in fact, moves a little farther away from Rodrigo. Resume on Alwa, sitting at his end of the row, looking embarrassed and disturbed; his eyes shift about restlessly beneath lowered lids.

Geschwitz, at the far end of the row, shifts uncomfortably away from Rodrigo and concentrates on the Defending Counsel's speech. The Defending Counsel raises his hand categorically and ends his speech for the defence:

TITLE: *No — this woman is no murderess . . . You must acquit her, for she is innocent!*

His concluding words are received with great sympathy by the public. They are even applauded. A few dissatisfied people, who protest against them, succeed only in increasing the noise.

The Presiding Judge repeatedly bangs a pencil on his desk.

Among the vociferous crowd cheering the speech, a well-dressed woman looks round, smiling confidently. She is distinguished to the finger-tips; a woman of good family.

Women all around her go on clapping enthusiastically.

The well-dressed woman gives a superior smile. She knows that Prosecutor's speech, yet to come, will soon put a stop to all this ill-bred emotionalism.

Lulu bends over from the dock and shakes her Counsel's hand, while he gallantly and demonstratively kisses her. She smiles warmly and thanks him.

Meanwhile, the Officers of the Court are still trying to restore order. The Presiding Judge points angrily at the public. This sort of commotion is not to be tolerated in a Court of Law.

Hastily the Officers of the Court order the public back into their seats.

Now that order has been restored, the Presiding Judge nods across to the Public Prosecutor.

The Prosecutor rises slowly from his seat, puts a cap on his head and closes the folder of documents in front of him. He retains only a small page of notes in his hand.

Lulu looks over at him.

70

He stands with the single sheet of notes and is about to begin when he catches sight of . . .

Lulu, who is smiling at him.

The Prosecutor begins his speech :

TITLE : *My Lords! Gentlemen of the Jury! The Greek gods created a woman — Pandora. She was beautiful — fascinating — mistress of the arts of flattery and infatuation . . .*

Lulu has become attentive. Her smile becomes more assured.

The Prosecutor sees this and guesses that Lulu is applying the words to herself. He loses the thread of his speech and stares across at her.

Lulu is smiling, gentle and forlorn. Her sweet face is touchingly framed by the black lace veil.

Lulu's smile confuses the Prosecutor . . . Already the pause is too long. He is suddenly aware of the moment. He tears himself free from this spell, [noticing with a start the disapproval of the well-dressed woman sitting in the public gallery].* With a jerk, he composes himself, and once again becomes the inexorable accuser.

TITLE : *. . . but the gods also gave her a container in which they enclosed all the world's evil. The heedless woman opened the box and all manner of evils were showered upon mankind!*

The Defending Counsel sits, leaning back at his ease, seemingly sure of his victory. He comments on the Prosecutor's excursion into the classics with a gesture which, translated into words, would be something like : ' Rubbish !'

The Public Prosecutor turns to face the Defending Counsel.

The Defending Counsel carries on smiling.

Then his expression hardens as . . .

The Prosecutor's smooth-shaven skull, with the little tuft of hair under the black cap, tightens; the face with its broad duelling scar creases into deceptively genial folds :

TITLE : *My learned friend, Counsel for the Defence, you cannot present the accused as an innocent victim of persecution. I tell you she is Pandora, for she was the cause of all evil for Dr. Schön!*

He leans back and takes his monocle out of his eye. With his left

---

* The Prosecutor's eyes do drift towards the public gallery at this point, although the well-dressed woman is not seen.

71

hand he pulls a silk handkerchief out of his breast pocket, breathes with wide-open mouth on the glass, cleans it, sticks it back in his eye, and turns with cold objectivity to the bench :

TITLE : *The arguments presented by Counsel for the Defence cannot shake me in my convictions. I have nothing further to add to the case for the prosecution. I therefore demand the death penalty.*

On these macabre words, a Reporter sitting in the Press benches swiftly lifts his camera and focuses it on Lulu.

A feeling of fear and horror compresses Lulu's throat. Her hands feel for the invisible something that is squeezing her gullet. She tugs at, and tries to loosen, the ribbon of her widow's bonnet.* But Lulu cannot get rid of the horrible sensation of choking. She feels the public staring at her with a thousand eyes. [She takes refuge behind her widow's veil which she draws over her face. The Presiding Judge turns towards her. With a friendly wave of his hand, he gives her permission to make a last appeal. Lulu stands up mechanically; she must lift her veil again.] She tries to speak. Not a sound comes from her lips. Resignedly, she gives in. Her hands drop, the veil falls back and hides the fear of death which begins to convulse her face. With her last strength, Lulu manages to shake her head, then she sinks down onto the seat. The black lace veil, caught in a current of air, wafts out dreamily before falling back over her distraught face.

At the Press table, all is activity. Pencils fly. [Two or three cameras are aimed at Lulu.] Beyond them, the Presiding Judge secures, with a look, the agreement of his colleagues. He stands up and adjourns the session. The Reporters are still feverishly taking notes as all the Judges stand up and withdraw.

The public gallery of the courtroom is seen from Lulu's point of view. It presents a formidable spectacle. The front row, spread right across the courtroom, holds the solid line of Lulu's friends. Behind them are row after row of benches, filled now with standing, moving, chattering people, all collecting their coats and hats and making for the doors.

In the hall, the recess releases a general commotion as the people

---

* The original script added here :
' The spectators crane their necks. Friend and foe stare at the accused. Now they have the sensation for which they have come. The well-dressed woman nods her head. Her satisfaction that immorality is meeting its just punishment gives something almost agreeable to her looks.'

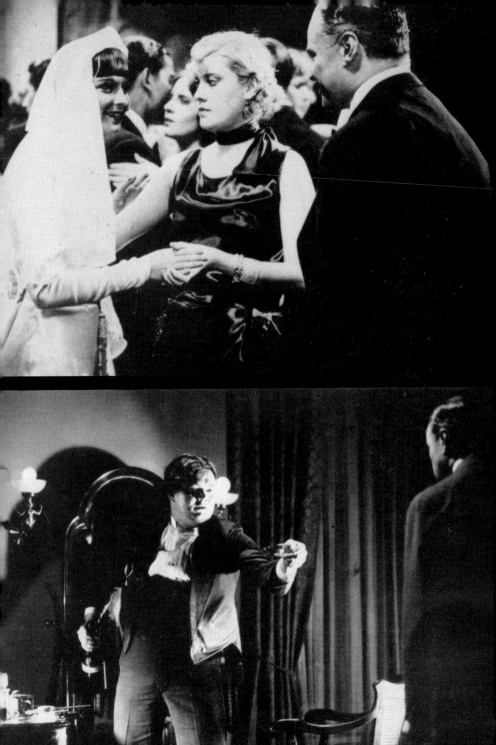

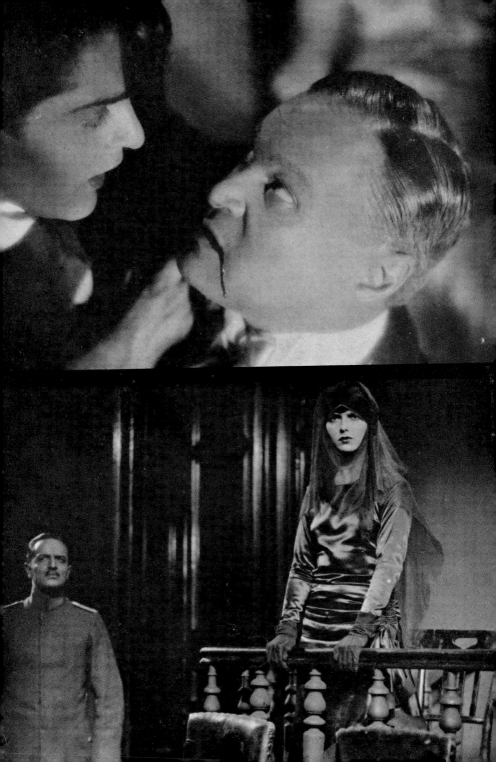

push and shove in their haste to get out.

In the courtroom, the Judges and Reporters gather up their respective papers and hurry out.

Amid all the coming and going, Geschwitz stands still and silent, her eyes fixed on Lulu.

Lulu is supposed to be led away by the two warders. She makes a few tottering steps, then her knees fail her. She would have fallen, if the Defending Counsel, who springs to her side, had not supported her.

Geschwitz is the only one in the courtroom who, throughout the proceedings, has taken Lulu's part with burning eyes and uncritical sympathy. Now the sight of the terrified Lulu breaks down her self-control. She tries to reach Lulu, to help her, to comfort her. She is, of course, prevented; kept within the limits proper to a witness by the guardians of public order. She is turned back, perhaps rather roughly and forcibly.

Meanwhile, Lulu is being helped to her feet by two warders.

Geschwitz tears herself from a warder's grasp.

She sees the Public Prosecutor standing among the public benches, conversing complacently with the distinguished lady.

She runs over to them.

Thoroughly affronted, they stare angrily at her.

Geschwitz bursts out :

[TITLE : *Mr. Prosecutor, I wonder what your wife would have become, if she had had to walk the cafés every night as a child!*]*

This outburst causes a small commotion. The Prosecutor gives a vigorous nod to the court attendants, and Geschwitz, amid mixed applause and disapproval from the public, is turned out of the court. She fights vigorously every inch of the way. Schigolch and Rodrigo come straggling up behind and follow Geschwitz out.

Only Alwa remains motionless in the midst of this disturbance. He sits there, his arms resting on his knees, his hands tightly clenched.

Two men and a woman energetically tackle the sandwich lunch they have brought with them. They talk excitedly between mouthfuls, hardly stopping for breath; agreeing, disagreeing, comparing, disputing, re-living the excitement, wondering : what will the ver-

---

* This title did not appear in the National Film Archive print in spite of the fact that Geschwitz shouts angrily at the Prosecutor.

dict be? And elsewhere, too, the lively debates begin. In short, this recess during Lulu's trial for murder has all the atmosphere of an interval at the theatre.

In the corridor outside, Geschwitz, Rodrigo and Schigolch are whispering earnestly together, looking round anxiously at the crowd. Schigolch goes over to small group and speaks with them. He turns his head back to look at . . .

Geschwitz, giving detailed instructions to Rodrigo, watched with interest by two young women. Rodrigo goes off. Geschwitz gathers the two women together and urgently whispers to them.

Two determined-looking men, wearing hats and belted raincoats, are standing in front of the fire alarm in the corridor. Rodrigo comes up and whispers to them. They nod grimly. He goes off.

People begin streaming back into the court from the corridor.

[The Beadle calls out a resumption of proceedings.]

The Judges appear and return to their places. The Presiding Judge nods to a warder to bring in the accused.

In the corridor outside, hundreds of people — crowding the entrance — are being refused admittance by the doorkeepers. This naturally gives rise to great indignation; it seems that scuffles might even break out at any moment. Conspicuous among them are two men — Rodrigo and Schigolch. They stand a little apart from the commotion, watching the throng anxiously.

At the bench, the Judges are standing, putting on their caps.

Lulu is now standing in the dock, a warder beside her. Her veil has been thrown back again; she is pale and stares at the bench. (Still on page 77)

The Presiding Judge begins to read the verdict and sentence from a sheet of paper:

TITLE : . . . *is convicted of manslaughter and I therefore sentence her to five years' penal servitude. She is remanded in custody for six months . . .*

Outside in the corridor, the crowding has reached a climax.

The two men we saw earlier standing by the fire alarm, peer suspiciously round the turn of the corridor.

One man, standing at the back of the crowd, is pushing with special violence. He pulls out a white handkerchief and, without turning round, makes a signal with it behind his back to the two men.

The man in front pushes the man behind.

He springs to the fire alarm box on the wall and smashes the glass [and pulls the handle].

His partner waves to him to come back quickly.

In the passage a few individuals, men and women, come running down the stairs, scattered apart.

Suddenly, the man who rang the fire alarm bell runs round the corner towards the crowd pressing round the doors. He starts shouting with terror-stricken gestures.

Meanwhile more people pour down the stairs.

In the tightly-packed crowd there are some who turn round to see. The man runs towards them with all the signs of panic.

Behind him, more and more people come crowding round the corner, with the same open mouths and the same terrified wide-staring eyes. They dash towards us and fling themselves wildly into the crowd. Clenched hands, bawling mouths, hats torn from heads, the face of a woman falling in a faint; all whirling round in one mad confusion . . . all is chaos, a fog torn apart by one cry :

TITLE : *F i r e !*

[The dazzling white letters of this word grow like lightning over the edges of the frame till finally nothing remains but meaningless white spots, flickering fragments of the letters.]

The people in the Courtroom have heard the commotion and are beginning to rise from the public seats. The Officers try to keep order.

The Presiding Judge and his colleagues are standing at the bench. The former has interrupted his reading of the sentence and is looking somewhat helplessly into the court. Then he reaches for the bell with his right hand and begins to ring it.

The crowd in the corridor surges against the doors.

The Presiding Judge rings more and more excitedly and vigorously his left hand waving the paper like a reassuring flag.

For now the doors to the corridor fly open. Through the narrow opening, irresistibly, like a mountain torrent, a knot of human bodies pours in, pushing against the excited mass of those in the court. These, maddened by the cries of terror from the others, press blindly against the doors. A boiling vortex is caused, which, after spinning for a moment in one spot, sweeps through the courtroom with the elemental force of an avalanche. Camera pans across with it as it rolls out, over barriers, benches, chairs. It treads underfoot any individuals who try to stop the panic.

Just missing our eyes, it presses past us, a confusion of distorted faces. It carries towards us a fluttering black speck, holds it before us, pulls it to and fro, until finally, amid the confusion, we see that it is Lulu. At this moment, Rodrigo pushes past behind her. He is shoving with superhuman strength through the mob, linked arm in arm with those eleven men who played as gladiators in the revue. A wall of men, they separate the warders from Lulu.* She stands in the midst of them. In vain the warders reach for Lulu across the rampart.

They are obliged to look on as she is swept away by the stream of people now passing across the screen. She vanishes. They themselves are almost carried away trying to hold back the stream which presses insanely onward, gradually becomes thinner, flows away. Now, all is emptiness before our gaze. Camera glides slowly back across the empty court, from the bench where the Judges stand bewildered to the well of the courtroom. In the space which a moment ago was a scene of raving animal terror, there is now nothing but destruction: broken barriers, bits of clothing, hats, overturned benches and chairs, scattered paper. And against the wall by the open door there leans just one man — Alwa. His eyes stare round at the incredible scenes. Then, a man comes across the court dragging behind him an unconscious woman; and after him another, spinning round and round like a madman . . . and laughing . . . laughing horribly . . .

[A Street.

Houses fly past us, lamp standards, advertisement kiosks. Cars pull over to the side in alarm; are passed. People stare at us. Before us are two fire engines, fully equipped with hoses and ladders. We bring up the rear of the procession in a crew car. The first engine bends sharply around the corner, shows us the full length of its

---

* It is not altogether clear from the film that the men in the crowd are Rodrigo's fellow gladiators, or that they are deliberately forming a wall by linking arms. This is all taken from Pabst's original script. The actual effect in the film is of a pushing, shoving crowd surrounding Lulu, and crowding her away from the warders whose job it is to guard her.

flank, disappears; then the second. Now we ourselves take the curve at full speed: in a broad bow the houses fall back to the rear, the square in front of the Courthouse presents itself to view. An excited crowd mills around outside the building. Out of the gates bursts the stream of fugitives. The fire engines have driven up at action stations, the crews have jumped off, and, in a purposeful, practised higgledy-piggledy, they are rolling out the hoses, elevating the ladders. Fade to:]

Alwa's Empty Room. The furniture and the piano are covered with linen dust-sheets. In the middle of the room there are two or three large closed packing-cases. On one of them we see two suitcases. Evidently everything has been arranged for a fairly long absence on the part of the owner, for the sun-blinds, too, have been let down — but not yet closed, so that the room lies in a twilight broken with stripes of light.
After a while the door opens. A black-clad figure enters, quickly closes the door behind it, and stays a moment leaning against the door, breathing deeply. It is Lulu. Then she goes over to a small table on which there are still a few things lying. Beside some cigarette packages, there are a travelling cap and gloves, a magazine, a railway timetable and a passport. Lulu hastily takes a cigarette, looks with nervous, unsettled movements for a light, finds one, and breathes the first, long-missed puffs deep into her lungs. This visibly calms her. She looks at herself in the mirror and adjusts her hat. Changing her mind, she takes off the widow's bonnet — the veil has already been torn away — and throws it down on a chair. Aimlessly, she turns and picks up the passport and the magazine, opening the passport with casual interest.
It is Alwa Schön's.
Lulu smiles contentedly and lays it back on the table. Then she looks at the magazine, leafing through it with a finger. She is deeply interested, wedges it hastily under her arm, looks around for somewhere to sit, then moves across the room. She goes over to the chaise-longue, and . . .
Stands by it for a moment, leafing through the magazine.
Then she makes herself comfortable on the chaise-longue and studies the magazine properly. (Still on page 78)
In the magazine, the new fashions naturally interest her the most.

Lulu flicks the pages happily.

There are also photographs among the fashion sketches, showing women in bathing costumes running along the sea's edge with the sunlit water behind.

Lulu suddenly has an idea. She jumps up from the chaise-longue . . .

And laying the magazine back on the table beside it, runs across the room . . .

And taking the way we know, running along the window gallery — now bare and desolate, all the flowers gone — she hurries on into . . .

The Bedroom, where she stops and stands . . .

It is completely dark, because the shutters are closed.

She turns on the light.

Before her, we see the marriage bed, see on the wall the baroque figure under which Dr. Schön bled to death.

Yet Lulu, with a quick movement, opens the wardrobe door and casts her eyes happily over the clothes still hanging there. She pulls out the fur-edged sleeve of a coat and smiles appreciatively.

One leaf of the door now conceals from her view the bed, the figure and her memories. Lulu stands with her face radiant before the clothes, which fill the inside of the tidy cupboard. With a light, almost dancing movement, she turns and hurries through the little wall door to . . .

The Bathroom, where the bath gleams, dazzling white and empty. [The brilliance of the room causes her to clap her hands in childlike pleasure.] In one bound Lulu springs to the bath and turns on the tap. She stands back again, out of sight, as the water gushes out in a broad stream.

The tap continues to run.

[In the street in front of the Courthouse, a fireman is just engaged in shutting off the hydrant and removing the hose. Outside the great gate of the building, groups of judges and barristers are standing. They are all robed. The officer in command of the fire detachment is just taking leave of them, saying, with a pretence of distress:

TITLE : *I am sorry to say, it was only a false alarm.*

None of them can help laughing.]

Slow fade to . . . Alwa's Room, where he is standing with his back to us, in front of the little table under the looking-glass. He picks

86

up the widow's bonnet in one hand, and swings round; his face shows his total astonishment. He turns about distractedly, his eyes searching the room, then he hurries, getting more and more excited, across to the door. Camera pans with him as he reaches it, halts a moment, then hurries out to . . .

[The Window Gallery. Alwa searches here, too. He comes up the stairs to the balustrade, and runs, as he sees the open bedroom door.] Alwa bursts through the bedroom door and dashes across the room. He sees the open wardrobe, and the clothes lying about, and he dashes on an excited impulse to the bathroom door. Unthinkingly, he wrenches it open. His right hand still on the door, his left propped against the door frame, he stands and stares into the bathroom. Then he abruptly shuts the door, turns and tears himself away.

He stops in the middle of the room, with his back to the bathroom door. He stands there taking deep, bewildered breaths.

After a very little while, the wall door opens and Lulu's head peeps through the crack. Her hair, still rather wet, hangs over her laughing face. Then the whole of her body slips through. She is wearing only a bathrobe wound closely about her, and she draws it provocatively round her body and walks happily across to Alwa.

He is still standing in the middle of the room. It is impossible for him to turn and face Lulu. She, for her part, now comes running up to him.

She taps him on the back. He still does not turn round.

So she leans her chin on his shoulder, smiling up into his face to attract his attention.

She pokes him in the back with her finger. He stiffens, but does not turn. Gently, Lulu pulls him round.

Alwa forces his eyes up to look at Lulu.

She smiles prettily at him.

Staring at her in silence, he at last manages to stammer :

TITLE : *How do you dare to turn up again . . . here?*

Lulu looks at him in frank astonishment :

TITLE : *Where else should I come, if not home?*

Alwa stares, amazed.

Lulu's sweet, smiling face is raised to his.

He is just about to lift up his hands to grasp the enticing Lulu, when he feels the widow's bonnet in his hand. And abruptly it drags him back into the terrible present. In helpless reproach, he holds out to her this token of horrible events.

But Lulu's untameable will to live is indignant at this link with the past. To her, it has become remote and indifferent; it no longer exists. With an angry gesture, she snatches the bonnet from Alwa's hand and flings it away.

The bonnet flies in a wide arc, [rolling across the bed, falling to the floor,] and crashes against the baroque figure in the very spot where Alwa's father died in his arms.

Seeing this, Lulu looks up defiantly.

Alwa's eyes are still fixed, in horror, at the bonnet and the spot where it has fallen.

He stares at the baroque figure, such a grim reminder of his father's death.

Alwa's hands clutch senselessly in the air. He snatches himself away from this woman and tears out of the room.

Lulu's glance follows the young man's flight; her expression is almost one of pity. Then she laughs, spins gaily round and runs back to the wardrobe.

She goes quickly to look at herself in the looking-glass. With a few fleeting tugs, she arranges her hair, adjusts the bathrobe in coquettish folds, spins round once more to admire herself, and then goes to find Alwa.

Alwa is standing in his room by the table where his passport and other articles of travel are lying. Hastily he puts them into his pockets. He looks up, startled, and camera pans quickly across to show Lulu standing in the doorway. She runs over to him.

[Alwa seizes his cap and gloves and runs towards the front door.] Lulu cuts off his escape. She reaches him at the door and holds fast his hand, which is already holding onto the handle. He wants to drag himself away from the spell of this hand and these wondering, questioning eyes, and he pushes towards her with the words:

TITLE: *If you feel at home where my father bled to death . . . then I must be the one to go away!*

She looks at him. Her head sinks sideways onto her shoulder, her hand slides from his arm. It seems almost as if she might totter and fall. Alwa is just about to catch hold of her to give her support,

88

when she warns him off with a nod; looks at him long and sadly, and quietly turns, going calmly to the other corner of the room. Alwa watches her from the door.

She goes across to the place where the telephone is. [She opens the book and begins to look for a number and, while she marks the place with the finger of her right hand,] her left hand raises the receiver to her ear and she dials a number.

Alwa has not left the room. He stares over at Lulu, not understanding her action.

Lulu speaks into the mouthpiece :

TITLE : *Is that the District Court?*

Alwa gives a start.

Lulu stares back at him deliberately, as he . . .

Still staring in horror at these words, starts to let go of the door handle.

Lulu continues speaking :

TITLE : *Please connect me with the State Prosecutor von Bodungen!*

She stands calmly waiting, the receiver to her ear. Then Alwa pushes into the picture. He is in a state of wild excitement. As Lulu vigorously resists, he snatches the receiver out of her hand. They struggle violently for it.

The State Prosecutor we have already come to know, is standing excitedly at his desk in his office. Three or four gentlemen with notebooks in their hands are standing before him. No doubt they are journalists. The State Prosecutor conceals his anguish behind a fulsome expression. Still continuing his lecture, he picks up the receiver.

Alwa and Lulu are struggling fiercely for possession of the telephone receiver. Alarmed by Lulu's loud protests, Alwa frantically covers her mouth with his hand. But Lulu will not give in; she fights back stubbornly.

The State Prosecutor has the receiver to his ear, and as he can get no reply, he presses the holder down several times.

Alwa is using all his strength in the desperate attempt to pull the receiver from Lulu's grasp.

The State Prosecutor presses the holder down again, impatiently, still continuing his statement to the journalists gathered round him.

Alwa holds Lulu away from the telephone with his right arm. He has at last succeeded. He himself speaks, breathlessly, but forcing down his excitement:

TITLE: *This is Alwa Schön speaking. Have you any news, yet, of that woman who escaped from the court . . . ?*

He listens, breathless with excitement, the receiver to his ear, then shakes his head and nods weakly, as if saying 'Thank you.' He drops the receiver down onto the table top, and stares with expressionless eyes into the void, until his head falls heavily onto his right arm against the table. Lulu smiles as Alwa collapses into a chair. She stares at him for a moment, then reaches for the receiver and takes it out of his unresisting hand. She lays it with a gentle, cautious movement on the stand. Now she feels safe. [She stands upright, a triumphant smile about her mouth. With an almost motherly, soothing gesture, she strokes Alwa's hair. A convulsive start goes through his body. Then she digs her fingers in his hair, lets it run playfully through them, and, as he still does not look up, she kneels down beside him. She lays her right arm about his shoulder and presses her face close to his, which is still hidden by his arm. So the two breathe cheek to cheek. (Still on page 78) Alwa's shame and resistance give way. He takes refuge in this forbidden embrace, squeezes himself up to Lulu in desperate anguish, trying to forget his misery and his conscience in long, burning kisses . . . Lulu frees herself from this outburst. While still in his embrace, she leans back her head and asks, with roguish certainty:]

TITLE: *Let's run away together. The Countess will lend me her passport . . .*

Quick fade to: the Corridor of a Sleeping Car, in motion. A hand opens a passport. The passport is made out in Geschwitz's name and bears her photograph. The hand turns over the pages until it finds the visa. A stamp is pressed under it and the passport is closed. [Now we see that we are in the Sleeping Car Attendant's compartment. The Attendant is standing before a boiling pot. He is preparing coffee.] A French Frontier Police Officer is stamping passports, leaning them against the wall, in a mechanical, indifferent fashion. He chats, meanwhile, to the Attendant [who has poured out a mug of coffee and offers it in a familiar way to the Officer.

He takes it with a friendly smile and begins to drink].*

The doors of compartments 6, 7 and 8 are shut. Alwa is leaning against the door of number 7. He is wearing a travelling suit and cap. He has, for the most part, mastered his anxiety, but his hands are clenched in his pockets.

A gentleman is standing in the narrow corridor outside the door of compartment 6. At this moment, the Customs Officials appear. The gentleman outside compartment 6 opens his door wide. [We see the open pieces of luggage lying on the unmade bed.] Then he steps back to let the Customs Officials go in. One of them does so, after asking the gentleman a question, to which he shakes his head in answer.

Alwa looks round nervously, casting his eyes furtively, a little desperately, in the other direction.

A Customs Official is approaching along the narrow corridor from that direction.

Alwa keeps his eyes on the Official, who comes up and salutes. And before the Official can knock on Lulu's door, [Alwa says:

TITLE: *The lady's luggage is in my compartment . . .*]**

The Official politely shrugs his shoulders, evidently excusing himself from having to do his duty. (Still on page 79)

So Alwa, after thinking for a moment, knocks on the door of number 7 himself. The door opens. The Official throws a fleeting glance into the compartment, doffs his cap politely and withdraws, shutting the door. He turns with a knowing but thoroughly discreet smile to Alwa, whom he invites with a slight, courteous gesture to open compartment number 8. Alwa does so, and when the Official enters, also follows him in.

The first Official has by now completed his examination of compartment number 6. The gentleman comes out of his compartment and stands in the corridor once again.

Meanwhile, the first Official comes past the open door of number 8 and moves on to number 9. Alwa's gaze follows him.

---

* In the film, the French Frontier Policeman is in the corridor, leaning on the outside wall of the Sleeping Car Attendant's compartment. The Attendant is half in, half out of the compartment, chatting to the Policeman and, no doubt, making coffee within, though this is not actually seen.
** This title did not appear in the film viewed, although the two men speak at some length.

The Official goes on down the corridor.

At this moment the door of number 7 opens. Lulu's head appears, an unlit cigarette between her upraised fingers. So far as we can see, she is not yet dressed, but is wearing over her pyjamas a Chinese jacket. She calls to Alwa.

He does not notice her, since his eyes are still fixed on the retreating figure of the Customs Official.*

Lulu is about to withdraw when she notices the gentleman from number 9 standing in the corridor, smoking.

Pertly, she asks him for a light and he reaches out his arm and offers her one from his cigarette. Lulu accepts with a thankful smile. She gives a quick look at the gentleman and shuts her door. The gentleman remains standing before the door. He becomes very thoughtful. Then, with a quick movement, he pulls a newspaper out of his pocket and, visibly excited, starts leafing through it.

He finds the page he has been searching for and his excitement increases. It is something like the excitement that the holder of a lottery ticket might feel when assuring himself for the second and third time that his number is that of the first prize. His glance wanders to and fro between newspaper and door. Then he nods, satisfied, tears half a page out of the newspaper and sticks it back in his pocket. He pulls out a fountain pen and, using the door of number 7 as a backing, writes something diagonally across the torn-out scrap of newspaper.

At this moment, Alwa appears at the compartment door. Uneasily he watches the gentleman's activity.

The gentleman has finished writing and returns his fountain pen to his pocket. He is now fanning the piece of paper so as to dry the ink more quickly.

Alwa stares in horror.

With an impertinent smile, the gentleman now takes notice of Alwa's presence . . . only to hand him the piece of paper.

Alwa, after a short, surprised glance at the gentleman, looks at it. The shock is so sudden that he cannot even begin to conceal it.

The piece of paper in his hand shows Lulu's photograph — taken at the moment in the courtroom when Lulu was vainly trying to say a last word — the headline informs the public that the authorities

---

* End of reel 3.

have offered a reward of 5,000 marks for Lulu's capture. Diagonally across the paper is written, in an energetic hand : ' Received with thanks. Marquis Casti-Piani.'

Alwa's dismay and perplexity are unconcealed.

So Casti-Piani looks pointedly down the corridor.

Alwa turns his head to follow his gaze.

There, farther down the corridor, the Customs Officials are still a visible threat.

Alwa looks at them. Then he gives a helpless look at Casti-Piani, who makes a slight warning movement of his head in the other direction, where Alwa now looks.

The Frontier Policeman is approaching, walking behind the Attendant who is carrying a tray with two or three cups of coffee on it. The Police Officer stops for a moment and makes a remark to the Attendant, who turns to look behind him. They exchange remarks. In feverish haste, Alwa pulls his wallet from his pocket, rummaging in it with shaking hands before passing some banknotes over to Casti-Piani, who accepts them elegantly. With a malicious smile, he smooths them out and goes back to his former position, leaning against the door of his own compartment. He quickly puts the banknotes into his own wallet [for the Policeman is just excusing himself for having to squeeze past the gentlemen. Alwa mutely lets him pass].

Now the Attendant also appears and stops in front of Alwa with his tray.

Alwa looks at him, unable to recover from the shock.

Casti-Piani handles the situation by taking the tray from the Attendant. Eagerly he knocks on the door of compartment number 7, which opens, revealing Lulu. Before Alwa can recover his self-command, Casti-Piani hands the coffee to Lulu with a winning smile. She withdraws to place the tray down inside the compartment. Lulu pops her head round the door and looks questioningly at Alwa . . .

He cannot avoid introducing the Marquis Casti-Piani to her :

TITLE : *Marquis Casti-Piani.*

Coquettishly, Lulu offers Casti-Piani her hand and he kisses it, respectfully it is true, but undoubtedly a moment too long. At that instant, a start goes through the group; the train has stopped. Lulu withdraws into her compartment, but leaves the door ajar. The Marquis smiles with pleasure.

Then he turns to look out of the window.

Outside, passengers, officials and vendors are all walking and running about on the platform. Alwa and Casti-Piani are leaning out of two neighbouring windows. While Alwa seems to be looking around for someone, Casti-Piani buys a big box of chocolates from a trolley. Alwa nods vigorously to two people who soon appear. They are Schigolch and Rodrigo, both carrying small hand cases. They are wearing travelling clothes which, despite their evident newness, have already taken on the characteristic marks of their owners. They nod up to Alwa and hurry past, while Casti-Piani turns away. [In the corridor of the sleeping car, Casti-Piani turns to Lulu's compartment. He pulls out the carnation which he is wearing in his button-hole and pushes it under the gold ribbon with which the box of chocolates is bound. Then he coolly pushes the door of number 7 open and, leaning right inside, hands Lulu the chocolates. Now Schigolch and Rodrigo appear in the corridor and loudly greet Alwa, who has trouble in concealing his distaste. The two of them also nod to Lulu, whom they can see over Casti-Piani's back. Lulu answers with enthusiasm. Casti-Piani turns, to find Rodrigo already offering him a great paw, which with some surprise he takes. Schigolch has pulled a small booklet from his pocket, in which he takes a quick look, then he bows to Casti-Piani and says:

TITLE : *Bon jour! Parlez-vous français?*

Casti-Piani laughingly makes way for the two.]

Lulu, sitting in her compartment, looks up and shrieks in delight. She holds out her arms to welcome Schigolch and Rodrigo as they push their way into her compartment and excitedly begin talking to her.

The train starts to move.

Alwa is standing morosely in the corridor. Casti-Piani comes up to him, taking out an expensive cigarette-case and offering him a cigarette. [Alwa hesitates for a moment, but Casti-Piani's face darkens with menace, so he takes a cigarette and accepts a light from the Marquis, who now benevolently puts his arm through Alwa's and draws him to the window. Here he takes a thoughtful puff on his cigarette, then says suddenly :]

94

TITLE : *May I prove my friendship by offering you some good advice?*

Alwa looks at him in silence. Then Casti-Piani pushes himself closer to Alwa, whispering almost in his ear :

TITLE : *Don't go to Paris. Too many eyes there. Come with me instead. I know a place where the people are hospitable . . . and know how to keep their mouths shut . . .*

We are on the Deck of a Ship. Over the remoter part of the harbour of a southern European city, the night sky glitters with stars. Close beside one another, sailing ships are lying at anchor, pointing their masts like fingers to the sky. On them, too, darkness reigns. Only the light buoys warn the few occasional boats of the obstruction.
On the deck of one of these ships there is a group of sailors. They squat together, inert, without a word. One is thoughtfully smoking a pipe, another cuts himself off a quid of chewing tobacco and shoves it in his mouth. The third tries to carve a sailing ship in the scanty light of a deck lantern. Somewhat apart from them, another man is sitting, weather-tanned and sporting a full beard. He is playing a plaintive mouth organ, while his right foot rocks a cradle. Under the thick bedding, the child is hardly visible. Behind him, a fat woman is taking a child's washing from a line.
None of these people takes any notice of a man, wearing a weather-beaten naval uniform, who is climbing over the ship's rail towards them. He helps a woman climb up onto the deck of the sailing ship from a small rowing-boat lying close alongside. Behind them a sailor bends over the rail to hoist up two or three suitcases. The couple stand on deck looking around them.
Meanwhile the sailors encourage the harmonica player to go on with his plaintive song.
The woman stands on the deck and looks round wonderingly. We can now see that it is Geschwitz. She turns to the uniformed sailor beside her in astonishment :

TITLE : *And Lulu's been living here for three months?*

The sailor nods eagerly, his face creasing into friendly folds. Grinning, he bends his face to hers :

Meanwhile the sailor now has all the luggage out of the rowing-boat, and has come up on deck. He takes the suitcases and follows Geschwitz and the uniformed sailor diagonally across the deck to a companion-way which leads into the interior of the ship.

A sailor in wide bell-bottomed trousers comes along the gangway. In one of his muscular arms he is holding a valuable champagne-bottle carrier. As he disappears down the next flight of stairs, Geschwitz and the sailor come down from the deck. It is dark [but the sailor has an electric torch with which he lights the way]. They walk down the gangway to the second companion-way, which leads still deeper into the ship. And here, the astonished eyes of Geschwitz encounter a smiling figure coming up the steps from below. It is Schigolch. He comes up to them and shakes hands, first with Geschwitz, then with the sailor who has brought her. Then he guides them back down the next companion-way, the way he himself has just come. Camera holds on them as they go down the second flight of steps, then tilts down to view them through the openings in the wooden steps. At the foot of the second companion-way we see for the first time a narrow passage. In the darkness, several doors show dimly on right and left.

The light of an open doorway shows two people coming from the other direction : a lady in evening dress, a gentleman in tails. They go happily through the open door into the warm light of the room within. The sailor with the suitcases follows them into this room. But Schigolch leads Geschwitz farther down the gangway towards a door at the end.

He opens this door and suddenly Geschwitz is blinded by the brightness of the light. She stands in the doorway, looking round. We are in a Large Saloon. Once, it may have served as a hold. The cross-beams and wall-ribs have remained raw and unpainted. The ceiling is low and heavy. In the middle of this room, flooded with bright light, men and women are crowding round a big gaming table. They are elegant, the women overloaded with jewellery. All races are represented : black, brown, yellow. And they are all concentrating, veiled in smoke, on the table and the game.

In the background a bar is installed. Among shining metal and cut glass and bottles, the barman is mixing cocktails. He is an old sailor, a fisherman from Iceland. The manager is leaning against the bar. His cap bears a captain's gold stripes. With brief looks he is directing the waiters of this room — all honest-looking sailors.

Schigolch points someone out to Geschwitz. She follows his gaze, nods happily and begins to move towards the crowd. Schigolch pushes her gently by the arm through the people who are standing squeezed around the table.

Among the crowd standing over the gaming table we can now see Lulu. She has changed her appearance. Like the others, she is in full evening dress and her hair is carefully arranged, but her only jewelry is a simple pearl necklace about her neck. She is standing intently over the seated Alwa as he concentrates on the game. His face is pale, his hair disordered, his eyes flickering feverishly about him. Geschwitz comes up and stands silently behind Lulu, watching. The game ends; Alwa has clearly lost again. Lulu turns round heavily, her eyes downcast . . .

She looks up to push her way past the obstructing crowd, and at first cannot believe it is true. (Still on page 79) She cries out in pleasure, stretching out her hand to Geschwitz to embrace her stormily. In the violence of this greeting there is more than just joy at seeing her again. It is like a sigh of relief, like a liberation from lasting strain.

Without letting go of Geschwitz, Lulu turns back to the table and jogs Alwa out of his infatuation with the game. He only turns and looks up at the two women with restless disquiet. He holds out his hand to Geschwitz, while turning back with feverish interest to watch the further progress of the game. Geschwitz sees with dismay the complete change in Alwa, then turns questioningly to Lulu.

Lulu can only shrug her shoulders with a short, bitter laugh :

[TITLE : *What do you expect? It's what we live on.*]

They refrain from continuing the conversation, [while Lulu helps Geschwitz out of her fur coat and hands it over to Schigolch, who then takes it away with the hat which Geschwitz also hands him]. Geschwitz puts her arm round Lulu's bare shoulder and leads her across to the bar, leaving Alwa to go on with the game. The other guests rapidly crowd round to fill the space thus left by Lulu and Geschwitz. [A young man is sitting on a high bar-stool in the company of one or two pretty cocottes. He is in tails like all the rest.]

97

At a table across the room, Schigolch and Rodrigo are celebrating magnificently with champagne. [Surrounded by a throng of spectators, a tall, powerful woman stands with her legs planted widely apart, and her arms stretched out. In each hand she is balancing a chair. With the chairs still in her outstretched hands, she begins slowly to kneel down.]* When she stands up again, Rodrigo leaps with his arms wide to embrace her. As he kisses her, groups of men are seen sitting on the chairs, pouring out champagne and drinking toasts to the enthusiastic, tumultuous, merry, half-drunken circle of spectators. But now, breaking away from this exuberant kiss, Rodrigo looks up and notices Lulu and Geschwitz, their arms round each others' waists, coming towards him. Flamboyantly, Rodrigo greets Geschwitz and kisses her hand. And, his breast swelling with pride, he points to the woman, goes and takes her in his arms and kisses her again before saying:

TITLE : *My fiancée! We're going to do a sensational Variety act!*

Lulu laughs, looks at the woman again and congratulates Rodrigo. He takes Lulu aside and, holding onto her arm, mysteriously whispers:

TITLE : *All we need is 20,000 francs to set the act up.*

[When Lulu tells him, with a shrug of the shoulders and a laugh, that she hasn't got a penny, he becomes ill-tempered and pesters her, barring her way and saying:

TITLE : *You must get me the money!*

But she hasn't got it! Rodrigo becomes angry; he must have it! Lulu is already trembling with agitation; can't he leave her in peace? She almost pleads with him, but he won't give way; he presses her, now almost threatening. Then she says, to get rid of him:]

TITLE : *Ask Alwa . . . maybe he won a lot of money today . . .*

[Rodrigo looks over to Alwa, but he is forced to make a sour face.] Alwa has just got up from the gaming table. From the distracted

---

* Although we do not see this display in the film, it has clearly taken place, and the crowd is congratulating the powerful woman.

way he leaves his place and detaches himself from the crowd, it is clear that he has lost everything.

[Rodrigo takes angry note of this and turns to Lulu, who laughs bitterly and tries to leave him. But he seizes her by the arm again and points stealthily. The young man at the bar-table is still staring at her, despite the fact that one of the girls, who is sitting next to him, is prodding him with her fork. But the young man clearly isn't paying her any attention, so she turns back, despondently, to the bar-table. Rodrigo whispers to Lulu:

TITLE: *The boy is stuffed full of money . . . be nice to him . . . and you can easily borrow the 20,000 from him . . .*

All at once Lulu becomes agitated and angry. Let me alone! She tries to tear herself free, and catches hold of Geschwitz's arm so that they may sit down at a table.]

Then Alwa comes up to Lulu, who forgets about Rodrigo as she looks urgently into Alwa's face. He draws her aside, trying to tell her something. Rodrigo's eyes show his smouldering anger as he watches them go. Geschwitz remains standing by the bar, biting her lip with excitement as she sees how Lulu is attacked from all sides. She stares at Rodrigo, alarmed by his inner violence and brute strength.

Alwa and Lulu come out into the gangway, where they stand illuminated by the light streaming out from the saloon. Alwa asks Lulu if she has any money. But she has none; he knows she has none! She couldn't give any to Rodrigo either! Alwa is unhappy. Staring hopelessly before him, he murmurs:

TITLE: *Damned bad luck . . . If I had some money to keep at it, I'm sure I could win it all back . . .*

For a moment Lulu just stands there looking at him, perplexed. Then she thinks of something. Her hand reaches for her pearl necklace and with a sigh of resignation, quickly, before she can find time to change her mind, she takes it from round her throat.

Just as she is doing so, Rodrigo's great hulking figure appears in the doorway; he looks on angrily as . . .

Lulu runs the pearls through her fingers, and, smiling as bravely as she can, holds them out to Alwa. Rodrigo's great hand comes down on her bare shoulder.

Roughly, he pulls her round and pushes her aside, reaching out at the same time for the pearls.

TITLE : *That scoundrel will pocket the lot!*

Lulu gets out of his way as he reaches again for the pearls. But Alwa resists angrily, putting them behind his back. So Rodrigo turns his anger on Lulu, repeating his words harshly to her. But she throws him an angry look : Stop that ! She knows who she can trust ! Before a full-scale row has had time to develop, Schigolch comes up to them from the companion-way; if he had not come between them Rodrigo would certainly have taken the jewellery. But Schigolch's black look works on Rodrigo like a hypnotic spell and the huge man slips back into the saloon, cowed by the powerful personality of the little man. Alwa can keep the pearls ! [Joyfully, with renewed hope, he takes them, and is about to hurry back into the room] when Schigolch seizes him, draws him aside and . . .
Leads him into the half-darkness of the gangway.
There he whispers to him with a tempter's smile :

[TITLE : *A clever man only gambles on certainties . . .*]

And secretively looking around him, he takes a pack of cards out of his pocket and tries to pass them into Alwa's hands. But Alwa repulses him with determination and tears himself free. Schigolch smiles confidently and puts the cards back in his pocket.
In a Small Cabin aboard ship, a photograph of an Oriental woman, stunningly dressed and posed, fills the screen. Suddenly, we realise that it is Lulu. A hand removes the photograph. Beneath it there is a similar photograph; this time, Lulu is posing in a low-cut, backless evening dress. The same hand removes this to show a third picture : Lulu as a belly dancer, her arms raised provocatively above her head.
We are in a sort of discreet alcove. An Egyptian is leafing through these photographs of Lulu. He makes a disdainful face and shakes his head, like a buyer who is trying to beat the price down.
Casti-Piani is drinking a cocktail through a long straw, looking up unconcernedly at the Egyptian. (Still on page 80) Coolly he raises his eyebrows :

TITLE : *What will you pay me if I persuade the girl to dance in your cabaret in Cairo?*

The Egyptian smiles shrewdly, as if to say : ' How much do you want? '

TITLE : *£300.*

The Egyptian makes a grandiose gesture, as if to say, with Oriental exaggeration : What! . . . Yes, £300, says Casti-Piani. The Egyptian jumps up, makes a demonstration :

[TITLE : *Not a first-class article, my friend . . . You are forgetting, the guests in my Cairo establishments are very fastidious . . .*]

The Egyptian protests : ' No, no; it's out of the question.' Casti-Piani lets him rant and rave; he doesn't give way. The Egyptian tries appealing to him as a friend, but no, Casti-Piani won't be swayed. Without losing his composure, and without taking his attention from his cocktail, he shakes his head, saying :

TITLE : *£300. Not a penny less. The police will pay me £250 any day I want it.*

The Egyptian flings himself back in his chair and ill-humouredly breaks off negotiations. He takes out a cigar and throws down the photographs. Casti-Piani gets up and leaves the cabin, leaving the Egyptian angrily striking a match.

At the gaming table in the Large Saloon, Lulu is standing behind Alwa; he is losing again.

Rodrigo comes up to a bald-headed man* who is counting out his winnings. He stands watching him silently for a while, scratching his cheek thoughtfully and smirking.

Lulu presses Alwa's shoulder to encourage him. But, superstitious like all gamblers, he turns irritably to her : Can't she leave him? She turns away, rather annoyed. [A little Japanese man squeezes up to her and secretively holds out a packet of counters : Why doesn't she play with these? But she resists his offer and escapes.] She goes over to where Rodrigo is now clapping the lucky winner on the back in fulsome congratulations. The bald-headed man smiles

---

* In the original script, the bald-headed man is referred to as the young man who was previously introduced, 'sitting on a high bar-stool'. For the sake of accuracy, we have followed the original script in calling him the young man in the scenes that do not appear in the film, and a bald-headed man in the scenes where he does appear.

and shows the beaming Rodrigo what a huge wad of notes he has won. Rodrigo's eyes glint. Suddenly he sees Lulu and calls her across, proudly presenting the little man to her. She is about to give him her hand when her attention is caught by the figure coming into the saloon behind her. She turns to see . . .

Casti-Piani, who comes in and stands for a moment in the open doorway separating the big room from the little alcove. Seeing Lulu at last, he calls to her.

She dashes over to him, laughing. He takes her arm to lead her inside and she goes ahead of him. As Casti-Piani follows her he nods meaningfully to a young woman who is standing alone by the wall. She gives a knowing little smile.

Rodrigo is having some success in latching onto the old man. He graciously introduces him to his fiancée. The little man seems delighted.

[In the Little Cabin, Lulu is hanging quite intimately onto Casti-Piani's arm and telling him, with repeated bursts of laughter, the funny story of what has just happened. Casti-Piani listens and exchanges a look with the Egyptian. The Egyptian nods in comprehension, now very interested, as Casti-Piani turns Lulu to and fro to show her to the Egyptian. Lulu does not suspect anything, letting him guide her as he pleases. The interested Egyptian comes closer and, without introducing himself, feels her in a businesslike fashion on arms and feet. Lulu stops laughing. All at once she becomes savage and hits him over the fingers. He is quite unmoved and doesn't even laugh. He turns gravely to Casti-Piani, draws him aside a little, and says:

TITLE : *All right, it's a deal. I'll just quickly get her a cabin on the ship and I'll be right back* . . .

They shake hands, not as a friendly leave-taking, but to seal the bargain. The Egyptian goes out, without a word of greeting to Lulu. Lulu gazes after him, half-laughing, half in astonishment. Then she really bursts out laughing and turns to Casti-Piani:

TITLE : *He behaves as if he were going to buy me!*

Casti-Piani nods quite seriously: You've guessed it! But Lulu does not believe anything so ridiculous. She snuggles up to him lovingly and tries to embrace him; but Casti-Piani quite firmly disengages himself and says categorically, but quietly, as if it were a matter of course :

TITLE : *I am in urgent need of money — and you and your friends have none left. The German police would be glad to pay 5,000 marks for you; my Egyptian friend is paying 6,000. So you're in luck . . .*

Lulu stares at him, her excitement mounting. But he lays a soothing hand on her arm and walks her round the room.]*
Casti-Piani is standing by the table. He takes Lulu's hand in his, and with his other hand taps out the bowl of his pipe. He declares in a matter-of-fact way :

TITLE : *And at the same time, I shall be providing for your future. The police will never find you in Cairo if you're with him at the Oikonomupulos establishment. They'll never dream of looking for you there . . .*

[Lulu's anger bursts out of her, but he bends over and whispers in her ear with an ingratiating smile :

TITLE : *And none but the very best people go there . . . rich foreigners . . .*]

He is holding both her hands now. Lulu snatches them from his grasp and screams wildly at him : 'No . . . no . . . it's not possible!' He can't do this!
[Her agitation finds expression in a burst of painful, almost convulsive laughter . . . She clings to his jacket, violently embraces him . . . But he quite calmly loosens her arms from around his neck and says :

TITLE : *None of that! I've already told you several times that you're not my type!*

He releases himself from her. She stares at him and drops her hands.]
The cabin door opens and the girl we had seen leaning against the saloon wall, the one whom Casti-Piani had given such a meaningful nod as he came by with Lulu, sticks her head in. She grins

---

* This scene in square brackets is taken from the original script. It was not seen in the print of the film viewed.

103

coquettishly at Casti-Piani. He goes across and puts his arm round her affectionately. The girl stands there, proud, challenging, triumphant. Standing with her in the doorway, Casti-Piani turns once more to Lulu, only to say brusquely :

TITLE : *Well, get changed quickly . . . you'll be leaving in an hour's time!*

He vanishes with the girl of his choice.

[Lulu stares after him, and a terrible, anguished cry bursts from her throat. In the doorway, Rodrigo now appears, pushing the young man into the room. The young man stands there, hesitant, comically bewildered, and yet fascinated . . . apologising . . . Rodrigo encourages him with a smile. Nothing to be afraid of! He arranges everything in a businesslike way, and rings the bell. Lulu stares at them, then bursts into convulsive laughter. She throws herself onto the sofa and invites the young man to sit beside her. He approaches, wild with happiness. With a thousand apologies, he sits down beside her, completely infatuated by her nearness and by the great quantity of alcohol he has drunk. Rodrigo gives orders to a waiter who has appeared, examining the wine list and ordering champagne. As the waiter goes obediently on his way, Geschwitz appears in the doorway, concerned about her darling Lulu. But Rodrigo springs towards her, seizes her by the arm and, kindly and cheerfully but yet roughly and energetically, drags her out. He does not want anything to disturb the couple . . .

In the Large Saloon, Rodrigo closes the door. He drags Geschwitz to the bar, to drink a cocktail with her. Suddenly his fiancée comes up and threatens to box his ears if he doesn't let go of this woman.

In the Small Cabin, the young man sits beside Lulu. She is childishly amused by him as he approaches her awkwardly and says, laughing:

TITLE : *I'm a student — travelling for my education . . .*

He feels her knee. Lulu defends herself, laughingly wildly. Two waiters come, serving a champagne supper. The young man is delighted. He snuggles up to her and whispers into her ear :

TITLE : *I've run away from my tutor . . . I wanted to enjoy myself . . . now he'll be hunting for me like a madman . . .*

He bursts into a fit of laughter, while the waiters serve wine and food without a flicker of an expression. They have the discretion of waiters in a private room, who have already heard, seen and experienced everything. The young man raises his glass and drinks Lulu's health. He drinks up, and all at once becomes quite wild. He seizes her and tries to throw himself upon her to kiss her, stammering, laughing with desire :

TITLE : *I'm travelling for my education . . .*

The old waiter fills up the glasses without concerning himself with what is happening on the sofa. There, Lulu is defending herself more and more angrily against the young man. She's no longer laughing now. She boxes his ears, jumps up and, with a word of abuse, leaves him. The second waiter now approaches the table and dishes up a large fowl. The young man, between the two waiters, gazes after Lulu.

Lulu storms out of the small cabin into the large saloon. She angrily slams the door. In a moment, Rodrigo is by her side, quite agitated : ' What's the matter then? ' Geschwitz also hurries up to her. Lulu clings, quite out of breath, to her dear friend, and hisses hysterically at Rodrigo :

TITLE : *You surely don't think I'll give myself to any casual boy!* . . .

She draws Geschwitz away with her. Rodrigo looks angrily, helplessly, at her. Then he looks round him and leans against the door. What can he try now? At that moment, his fiancée comes up and pokes him in the ribs. He has a saving notion. He whispers with her for a moment and pulls her to the door.

The young man is sitting unhappily in the small cabin, pouring one glass after another down his throat. He looks up in alarm as Rodrigo comes in with the gigantic lady. He jumps up and is introduced. He manages to kiss her hand, despite his alarm. She sits on the sofa; draws him down beside her with an ingratiating look. The young man gazes round helplessly, suddenly finding himself almost sober. So he tries to stand up. But Rodrigo is standing on the other side of him, and he fills the young man's glass again and, wishing him a pleasant evening, leaves him to the tender mercies of his fiancée. She reaches for the fowl and begins to eat, overwhelming the terrified young man with endearments.]

Geschwitz is standing in a corner on the Deck of the Ship, watching

. . . Casti-Piani, who comes by with his new girl on his arm. All at once, Lulu comes tearing after them. She manages to seize him by the shoulder and turns him round to face her. He pushes her off, but she grabs at his jacket.
She pleads with him : 'You can't send me away! You can't!' The tears are streaming down her face :

TITLE : *I won't go with him!*

How can she make him relent? How can she make him see her agony? She clings to him in despair, but coldly he removes her hands from his shoulders. Her tears mean nothing to him. She stands there a moment, helpless. But he insists :

TITLE : *I need the money. If you're not ready to leave in an hour's time, I'll call the police.*

[She bursts out :

TITLE : *I cannot sell myself! That would be worse than prison!*

He gives a scornful laugh. Geschwitz dashes forward to protect Lulu from him. Casti-Piani only looks at her contemptuously, then bows scornfully and turns to Lulu with the polite question : 'Well?' Again, Lulu gives a decided, hysterical : 'No!' And yet, she is imploring, pleading : 'No, I can't!' But he is cold, and a cruel grin spreads across his face, almost concealing his rage.]
Lulu stares at him, pitifully.
With a scornful look, he turns to go.
Lulu cannot believe it; she stares after him in horror.
Geschwitz has witnessed this whole terrible scene. Now she stands clutching her handbag, lost in thought. She looks over at Lulu.
The poor, lost creature has her fingers to her lips and is staring all about her in anguish. Her eyes are so filled with visions of her hideous fate that she does not even see Geschwitz.
Geschwitz, normally so strong, looks at this sight, and her eyes fill with pity.
Lulu shakes her head mindlessly, dumb with horror. She hardly knows what she is doing. She has only one person left who can save her. She must go to Alwa! She turns and flies back to the saloon.
Suddenly Geschwitz has an idea. She opens her handbag, checks how much money she has in it, and hurries off after Lulu. There is

a look of determination on her features.

Alwa is sitting at the gaming table in the Large Saloon. There is not a single counter in front of him. He is in a state of complete collapse, staring apathetically before him. He doesn't even have the energy to get up.

Geschwitz has arrived and is staring over at Alwa from the bar.

And now Lulu makes her way through, pushes up close to Alwa and bends down urgently to say something in his ear. He doesn't reply, and in a moment she sees that he has lost everything. Suddenly a man standing beside Alwa presses him to get up if he is not playing. Alwa is roused from his apathy and gives up his place. He hasn't even noticed Lulu's presence.

But she takes hold of him and leads him from the throng of gamblers. They go up to Geschwitz, who is sitting on a high bar-stool. While Lulu talks to her, earnestly, Alwa keeps glancing back at the table.

And then Rodrigo, who is sitting farther along the bar, sees . . . Geschwitz reaching down and slowly taking some banknotes out of her handbag; all her money. And she offers it simply to Lulu, who holds the crumpled notes in her hand.

Rodrigo gapes, disgruntled.

TITLE : *2,000 marks . . . it's not enough . . .*

But Alwa is staring greedily at the money, fired with new hope. Lulu cannot help but notice. Very well; she presses the money into his hand — at least he can try to save them. With a joyful expression he is about to return to the table, but she holds him back.

As she looks up at him, her eyes fill with tears; only he can save her now !

Alwa is counting the money feverishly.

She implores him :

TITLE : *Alwa, you've got to win! You must win, Alwa . . . you must . . . or I'm finished . . . !*

He looks at her. Then thoughtfully he looks round the room. He understands. Seeing Schigolch by the wall, he goes over to him and takes him out to . . .

The Gangway, where they come through the door. Alwa draws Schigolch aside. [He looks round fearfully and draws him farther away round the corner.] Then he stops. He wants the cards. Schigolch

smiles with understanding, takes the cards from his pocket and pushes them into Alwa's hand. Alwa furtively pushes them inside one of his sleeves and slinks away, back into the saloon. Schigolch is content.
[Lulu is standing at the door, quite anxious, as Alwa comes up, full of hope again : he'll do it now!]
Rodrigo comes over to Lulu, angrily :

[TITLE : *You've given him money again . . . hand it over!*]

Lulu turns away from Rodrigo and hurries off, leaving him staring after her.
[Rodrigo holds Lulu back and says, clicking his teeth with rage :

TITLE : *Very well then . . . but I'm telling you, if you haven't got the 20,000 francs by this evening, I'll denounce you to the police!*

But he notices Schigolch coming up, so he strolls off. Schigolch is now standing beside Lulu and notices her terrible agitation. He speaks to her, trying to calm her, but this makes her break out in even more hysterical sobbing. He tries to comfort her, but she tears herself free and dashes down the corridor. He trots after her, quite excited.]
At the gaming table in the Large Saloon, Alwa holds the bank. He is winning. He counts out several notes for his next bid and throws them into the croupier's tray.
Lulu is now in the Companion-way, where Schigolch is holding her in his arms, trying to comfort her. She drops her head hopelessly onto his shoulder. Concerned, he gently pulls her down with him as he sits on the stairs, saying : ' For heaven's sake what is the matter with you? '
Lulu looks down at his kind face and slowly sits down on his lap. She cannot take any more.
Slowly she sinks her head on his shoulder, as Schigolch pats her arm reassuringly.
He comforts her, and she bursts out, a poor, wild creature hunted to death :

TITLE : *Everyone . . . everyone wants my blood . . . my life . . . they're sucking it away . . . horrible!*

She sobs and cries : ' Money, money, money! That's what they're all after ! Nothing but money !' When she raises her head, her eyes

are filled with mortal hate.
Schigolch just holds her in his arms like a little child and strokes her tenderly :

TITLE : *Have a good cry about it, my pet. Just cry your heart out!*

She sobs, and then pulls herself tearfully away from his shoulder.

TITLE : *Save me! That Sampson, Rodrigo, wants to turn me in . . . Save me!*

Desperately she looks into his face.
Schigolch's face becomes distorted. He puts his pipe between his lips and puffs grimly : ' Him ? ' ' Yes, yes, Rodrigo.' Unexpectedly, Schigolch's eyes fill with tears. Grimly he says :

TITLE : *I'll fix it.*

He looks up at her; her eyes are fixed far away. He pulls her to him, questions her, gives her instructions. They make plans. Suddenly Lulu is anxious, she has heard a sound.
They get up quickly and Lulu goes back to the saloon. Schigolch puts his pipe back in his mouth and climbs heavily up the stairs.
On the landing above, Rodrigo is just coming along the gangway, down from the deck. He is about to go down the next flight when Schigolch appears below him, coming up the other way. He smiles up jovially. Leaning across the barrier, he pulls the huge man down to him and whispers :

TITLE : *I know a way to get us all out of the soup!*

Rodrigo is interested, so Schigolch pulls him down by his sleeve and whispers mysteriously :

TITLE : *Geschwitz is mad about you, and she's got money . . . It was only because of you that she travelled after us . . .*

Rodrigo won't believe this ! He laughs at the joke.
But Schigolch swears it's true. He pulls Rodrigo down to him again. The vain, strong man takes fire as Schigolch, his eyes gleaming, insists :

TITLE : *She's got money . . . You could easily lure her into our cabin . . . and if you're nice to her, she's sure to get her money out . . .*

The little man gives an ugly laugh and Rodrigo laughs with him —
but no, he makes a face: she's not his type. Schigolch laughs at him
. . . and he nods, and gradually yields . . . Schigolch starts to
go backwards down the stairs, drawing Rodrigo after him with his
eyes. After another, almost bashful shrug of the shoulders, Rodrigo
lumbers down behind him.

In the Large Saloon, Rodrigo's fiancée clears a path for the bald-
headed man, through the crowd at the gaming table. He follows
her, both hands full of counters. She won't let him go. When they
reach the table she sets him down in an empty chair beside Alwa.

In another corner of the saloon, Lulu is whispering urgently to
Geschwitz:

TITLE: *You're the only one who can save me!*

She clings desperately, persuasively to her (Still on page 80), fondly
stroking her arm:

TITLE: *Rodrigo is madly in love with you!*

Just then Rodrigo appears at the bar, followed by Schigolch, and
they both order large drinks.

Geschwitz starts back at Lulu's words: 'No, that can't be!' She
catches sight of Rodrigo across the room and resists with all her
might.

Standing at the bar, Rodrigo pats his hair into place in the mirror.
Schigolch is still urging him on. Rodrigo turns, and seems to catch
sight of Geschwitz and Lulu. The sight of them makes the great
hulking fellow giggle and turn bashfully round again.

Geschwitz is trembling with agitation. But Lulu begs, implores her
in desperate whispers. She begins to weaken under Lulu's pleading:

TITLE: *Throw yourself at him . . . He'll do anything for you,
anything you want! Otherwise he'll blab on me, he'll get the
police . . . !*

[Rodrigo appears and approaches her. Disgust overcomes Geschwitz. He comes up to them, greets Geschwitz with an ingratiating
and seductive smile, takes her arm and draws her away, with an
invitation on his lips. Going over to the bar, he gives an order. Like
an accepted lover, he won't let her go. Schigolch exchanges a look
with Lulu, then he steals out. Lulu gives a sigh of relief and looks

over at the bar.]
Rodrigo is pressing Geschwitz to drink with him. She stands in front
of him, holding the drink up awkwardly to her face. She gives one
last, imploring look at Lulu, like a lamb led to the slaughter, but
then, forcing a gay smile, she sacrifices herself, and drinks.
From across the room, Lulu implores her again, her hands anxiously
clasped.
With forced gaiety, Geschwitz manages a seductive laugh for Rodrigo. He is convinced. He drags her away with him.
Relieved, Lulu turns to the gaming table. And suddenly, she smiles.
She presses close to Alwa and looks on with shining eyes. Camera
pans along and tilts down, past the crowd of onlookers and players
at the table, past the croupier drawing in the winnings, and holds on
Alwa. He is unmistakeably winning. He is quite joyful, completely
changed. Camera holds on his face for a moment, then tilts farther
down, past the sweat pouring from his temples, to the table where a
great quantity of banknotes and counters is piled up in front of him.
Lulu laughs with pleasure. She is saved.
She runs across to the bar, not noticing that a cabin boy, holding a
tray full of glasses, is standing close to her and gazing at her with
eyes of love. Then she looks at him. [He becomes confused, turns
away his face and tries to escape.] Lulu laughs aloud, pleased that
the boy is so infatuated. She stretches out her hand, takes a glass
from the tray and drinks it down, flirting with him. At last she is
her old self again.
In the Gangway outside a Cabin Door, Rodrigo is standing with
Geschwitz. Half-rough and scheming, half-excited himself, he seductively pulls the woman towards him. She now shows her total disgust.
Inside the cabin it is quite dark. Schigolch is sitting, listening for
every sound. Suddenly he draws back into the darkness and hides
behind a heavy curtain, for the door is opening. Geschwitz comes
backing into the room, pulling Rodrigo at arm's length in after her.
He shuts the door without letting go of Geschwitz. Then, violently,
he snatches her to him and throws himself on her in uncontrollable
passion. (Still on page 113)
In the Large Saloon, Lulu has become serious. She slowly turns round
to look at Casti-Piani, who is standing behind her and is bending
over to speak in her ear. He turns to lead her away, but Lulu has
recovered her control now. She smiles confidently and merely directs

her gaze across to the pile of money lying before Alwa. Camera pans across the table, past the players, to show Alwa being handed yet another tray full of notes and counters.

Greedily, he adds them to his pile.

[Lulu says with a triumphant laugh :

TITLE : *Don't be afraid . . . you'll have your money soon . . . my dearest!*

Casti-Piani looks and bites his lip. Alwa is now quite merry and begins the last deal. He deals to the young man, who has already lost practically everything; but the woman acrobat is still urging him on.]

A man with a very set expression on his face is leaning over Alwa.

Alwa is about to deal the remaining cards. Suddenly a hand reaches down and grips hold of his hand with the cards in. It is the hand of the man who is leaning over him; a fierce-looking crook. Alwa resists him in terror, but he takes his hand firmly. (Still on page 113)

With no effort at all, he pushes Alwa's other hand away . . .

And reaches purposefully into Alwa's sleeve. It is all over for Alwa. He has given up struggling now.

The man slowly takes out several cards from Alwa's sleeve. With a knowing smile he holds them up for all to see.

Alwa cringes beneath the man's grip, staring, wide-eyed with horror; the shame of being exposed presses down on him.

There is general excitement. The people stand up, they press around. Lulu comes running up, her head just visible in the crowd around Alwa. Revealed as a cheat, Alwa jumps up and defends himself against the accusation. He hardly knows what he is doing. He pushes the crowd back in a desperate effort to gather up his winnings. But the crook grabs his arm and locks it behind his back, holding Alwa pinned down to the table.

Lulu screams. But now, her fate is sealed. Casti-Piani appears and pulls her forcibly away from the table. He drags and pushes her over to the door and shoves her out ahead of him. Guests are rushing madly across the saloon. Someone shouts out :

TITLE : *Police!*

With a huge effort, Alwa manages to pull himself free.

His entire body sprawls itself across the table in his efforts to free

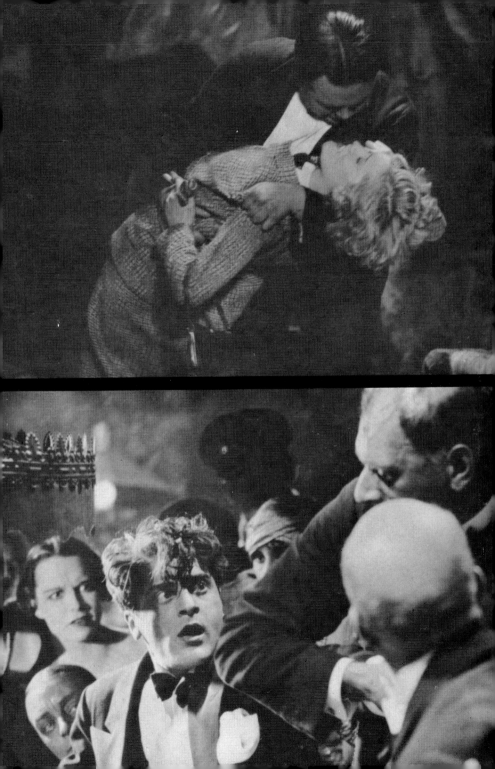

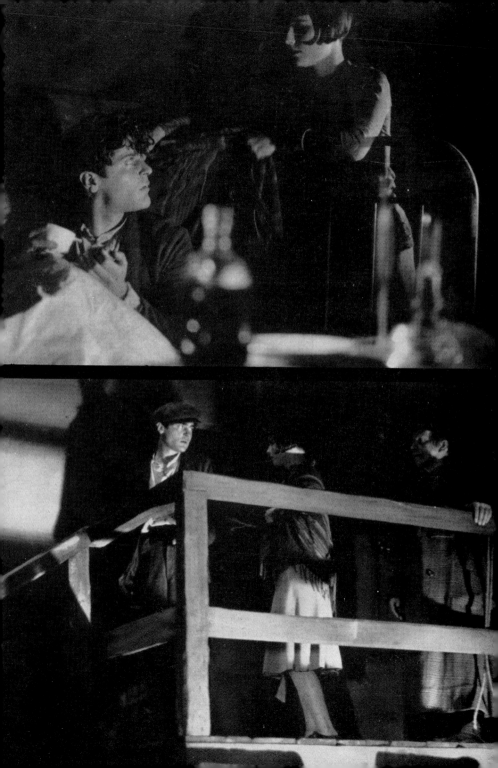

NOTICE

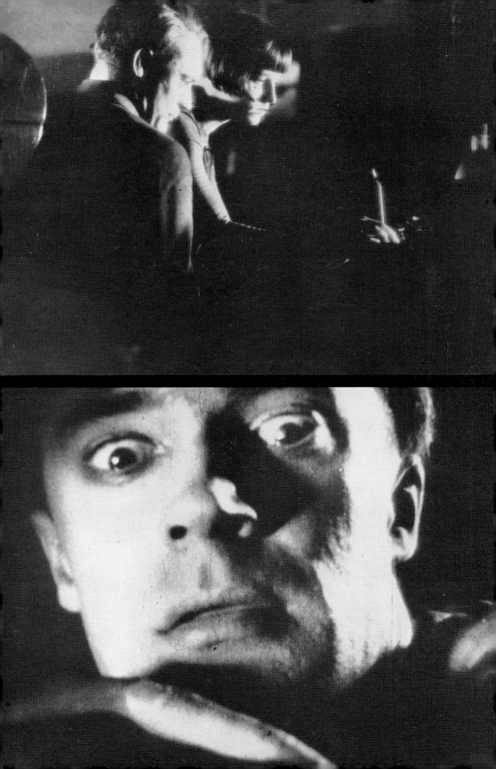

himself completely and grab as much of the desperately needed money as he can. But his two hands are seized from behind him, and he is pulled right away from the pile of notes. Now whole crowds are pressing round the table, every man for himself, while the croupier's rake comes across the table in a hasty effort to retrieve the money.

Casti-Piani pushes Lulu up to a doorway where the Egyptian is waiting for her. She fights desperately : she won't go with him ! But her feeble strength is nothing against the two men, and she is thrown into the cabin.

Tumult has broken out in the Saloon. Several sailors look on, unperturbed, perhaps even a little amused, as the guests shove each other in their greediness to get what they can from the table. Alwa is grabbed by several pairs of hands, and camera pans across the saloon to the door as he is flung out.

Bodies push bodies, hands fight with hands grasping money from the table. The saloon is in uproar. The chaos increases now as several people try to push out away from the table, their hands full of crumpled notes. Greedily, guiltily, they hold the bills up to their faces to count out how much they have managed to grab.

They waste no time now in hurrying from the table.

Amid the hubbub, Rodrigo's fiancée is arguing fiercely with the one-time winner, trying to console him. But he wants his money ! He has been cheated ! Angrily he shouts at her . . .

He won't be silenced : he has been cheated ! He storms back to his table shouting :

TITLE : *The police! The police! I'll call the police!**

In the Small Cabin, Lulu is sitting on a chair in a state of complete collapse. Casti-Piani is standing over her, smoking a cigarette, cold, cynical : ' Well ? ' She doesn't move. And he becomes more and more irritated.

In the Large Saloon, the tumult over the money continues. The young man is whimpering hysterically : ' Give me my money back !' The Amazon helps him, screams with rage, and tears several men away from the table, but she is pushed back by the others. The young man becomes aggressive, and again threatens to call the police.

---

* End of reel 4.

Two of the guests now seize him and throw him out, amid encouraging laughter from the men around. The young man springs back and shouts:

TITLE: *Police! I'll call the police!*

Then he is angrily seized and thrown out again.
In the Cabin Gangway, the young man comes running past, shouting: 'Police!'
Lulu still sits unmoving in her chair. The Egyptian is now ready to leave. Casti-Piani nods to him: In a moment, then. He shakes Lulu: It's time. She must go. But Lulu raises her head and defends herself with dazed energy, convulsively: No! No! No! She won't go! She can't! Casti-Piani rages, and lifts the telephone receiver with the threat:

TITLE: *Then I'll call the police!*

Lulu jumps up, bursting out: 'Call them! Call them!' She tears herself free and runs out, frightened to death, not knowing where she can go; but only knowing she must run, run somewhere, anywhere away from this hell that awaits her. Casti-Piani raves while the Egyptian springs at him and takes the telephone from his hand: Surely, he's not really going to call the police? Casti-Piani gives an angry, savage laugh:

TITLE: *I don't want to have anything to do with the police . . . But the threat is enough . . . in two minutes she'll be back . . .*

He throws himself into an armchair and angrily smokes his cigarette.
In the companion-way, the young man races up the steps shouting: 'Police!'
Back in the cabin gangway, Lulu drags herself forward in a state of complete despair. Suddenly a cabin door opens in front of her, and Schigolch glides out through it. He shuts the door again and locks it with a key. Lulu stares at him, while he nods: All in order! Then in great haste he adds:

TITLE: *But now as quick as you can . . . I'll get a boat . . . I'll be waiting for you by the anchor . . .*

Lulu nods, half in a daze, as he runs away. She moves a little farther on, then stops outside another cabin door, looking around

122

her. There, standing in the corner and staring at her, is the cabin
boy who has become so infatuated with her. He stares at Lulu with
the same love in his eyes. She nods to him, and he runs up. She
opens the door and pulls the boy inside. The door shuts.
On Deck, the sailors' rest is disturbed. The young man runs to the
ship's rail and shouts:

TITLE: *Police! Police!*

The sailors come to him and try to control him, but he gets wilder
and wilder and goes on shouting.
Alwa is dragging himself along the deck in complete despair. Now
he has made up his mind. There is only one thing left for him — he's
going to throw himself into the sea. But Schigolch catches hold of
him. Alwa resists: he wants to die, he has nothing to live for now.
But Schigolch draws him irresistibly away.
The young man breaks loose from the two sailors and shouts:

TITLE: *Police! Police!*

A third sailor joins them and shouts: 'Throw him into the sea!'
So the two others catch hold of the young man and throw him in.
The young man sinks in the sea. The sailors withdraw from the rail,
like men who have done their job well.
The young man comes to the surface. He flails around desperately,
his arms beating at the water. Still he is shouting:

TITLE: *Police!*

A beam from a searchlight picks him out as he goes under again.
The beam hunts around for him. He comes up again and calls out
more and more desperately as he struggles against drowning:

TITLE: *Police!*

He goes under again. The light beam casts around, searching for
him.
Policemen on a Police Motor Launch are hunting with the powerful
searchlight. A little man shouts: 'There he is!'
Picked out by the searchlight, the young man can be seen fighting
desperately with the waves, almost underwater now as his strength
flags. Then the motor launch comes alongside him and, just in time,
he is rescued.

He is hauled on board the motor launch. The little man, who is his tutor, cries out:

TITLE: *Your Highness* . . .

The young man is surrounded. He tells his story and points, more and more breathless, dripping wet and cold: 'There . . .' The order is given, the launch moves off.

The launch draws up alongside the ship.

On the Ship, several sailors, frightened for their lives, are running across the deck. Policemen in plain clothes jump aboard. A cabin boy helps them up, one after the other. They all carry revolvers and powerful torches. They run to the companion-way. The cabin boy turns towards them. It is Lulu is disguise. She hurries diagonally across the deck. And looks down over the rail. A boat is waiting below. Alwa is sitting inside it. And now Schigolch helps Lulu climb aboard.]

The Cabin Gangway is thronged with people; the guests are racing *en masse* to reach the steps leading up to the deck. Suddenly they stop.

They cannot reach the steps because now the police have come down and have cut off their escape. These huge, powerful men look threateningly at the crowd; the guests all now have to prove their identity to the police.

[Casti-Piani is among them. He speaks with a Policeman, then calls out: 'There!' In an open cabin door, a figure wearing Lulu's dress flees towards the companion-way. Casti-Piani calls out: 'There she is!' The Policeman blows his whistle, and the woman is seized by two other Policemen. The torches light up the woman's face. He laughs aloud, childishly, comically, for it is not a woman at all, but the cabin boy. Enraged, Casti-Piani tries to attack him, but the cabin boy gives him a right hook to the chin which knocks him senseless. There is laughter at first, but suddenly everyone's attention is on the scene in the other direction.]

In the dark Sleeping Cabin, Geschwitz is kneeling at the door and banging desperately upon it. Frantic now, she at last manages to tear it open.

Outside the cabin door, the crowd and the policemen all stand rooted to the spot, staring wide-eyed.

The cabin door is broken open. Geschwitz almost falls out. Half-mad, still on her knees, she points to the interior of the cabin. The crowd surge upon her, and two strong policemen take hold of her limp, hysterical body and pull her away.

The crowd all shove against each other round the open doorway. The Chief Policeman pushes through them, and stops dead at what he sees.

Shining horribly in the light of the torches is the dead face of Rodrigo. The eyes stare up vacantly from the floor of the cabin.

On the sea, among the ships, Alwa and Schigolch are rowing with all their strength. Lulu sits in the boat, still dressed in her sailor suit, staring in front of her.

TITLE : *We'll have to try and get a boat going to London!*

They pull out into the open sea, rowing with all their might.

Fade in to a Slum Street in London. [Through thick winter fog, shadows pass. Only their movement betrays that they must be people. From somewhere an invisible street-lamp squeezes a faint beam of light through the swathes of fog.] A shadow approaches, slowly assuming a shape. As it crosses the wedge of light, it becomes visible as a human face.

The shadow comes nearer, to reveal the face of a man. He is walking aimlessly through the indifferent streets, wearing nondescript clothes, and despite the winter cold, only a thin overcoat protects him. This face passes through the fog, going slowly, having nowhere in particular to go to. Camera tracks out in front of the face. The man's eyes flicker unsteadily, without a fixed object. [Once, near to some source of light, a woman's face approaches in a bold invitation. The effect is startling; the man's eyes become fixed and, filled with some fear, he hastens on.] Once more he plunges into shadow and fog, until suddenly he enters a circle of light which forms a warm, bright ring in the fog. The man turns his face to this light, and camera pans with him as he moves across to it.

The light is coming from a low, uncurtained window, which gives a glimpse into the interior of a room. There, in the warmth within, parents, children and friends are gathered around a lighted Christmas tree. The men hold steaming glasses in their hands, the women are being children with the children.

The man turns up the collar of his overcoat. This glimpse into the secure warmth of a family room makes him feel cold for the first time. He walks on. The fog swirls round him. Figures pass; engrossed in their thoughts or deep in conversation, they hurry by; they have somewhere to get to, destinations to head for, out of the fog and cold.

The man goes round a corner and stands in front of a small square, cosily ringed by houses. It is brightly lit, for a Salvation Army group is in possession of the corner. The musicians play and blow, a few women sing. But the interest of the twelve to fifteen poor souls, standing in a ragged circle about the square, (Still on page 114) is concentrated on the tea-urn, from which two young girls are filling mugs of tea. They hand the mugs round and distribute big pieces of cake with them as well.

The man stops. Motionless, he observes the scene.

His eyes take it all in, from the musicians in the one corner, across to the groups of destitutes, and finally they come to rest on two or three old women huddled round their mugs of tea.

Here his eyes fasten on someone.

It is one of the young Salvation Army girls, who is busily engaged in distributing tea and cake to the old women. She looks up and sees the man watching her. She falters under the intensity of his gaze.

His eyes are burning as he gazes silently upon her.

The girl is holding a last mug of tea in her hands. Slowly she comes towards him.

She offers it to him.

Still silent, he takes it from her, putting both his palms around the mug to get the full warmth from it.

His eyes do not leave the girl for a moment.

She looks at him, her eyes wide with compassion.

His expression is fixed on her.

A little disconcerted, she lowers her gaze.

Suddenly he digs into his pockets, brings out all the money he has on him, and . . .

Hands it to the girl.

She takes it, smiling easily with thanks, and goes straight over to throw it in a pot which stands on a tripod in the middle of the group. Above it is a huge, hand-painted sign, reading: ' Old Ones' Xmas.' The girl looks back once more at the man.

He stands with his back to her, then starts to walk slowly away.

126

She goes up to him.

He is standing in front of the big Christmas tree. She taps him lightly on the arm, and he turns, surprised.

She is looking up at him with big, humane eyes. Softly she says:

TITLE: *We only take in order to be able to give again . . . How can I help you, brother?*

[The man pushes the mug at her with both hands.] He gives a twisted smile and shakes his head roughly, scorning her aid:

TITLE: *Nobody can help me! I cannot be helped!*

He starts to move away. But, again, she stops him lightly with a gentle touch on the arm, and taking a sprig of mistletoe from the tree, hands it to him.

Wonderingly, he takes it from her.

She stares up at him.

He puts the mistletoe inside his coat. Then, without a word, he moves off slowly, and plunges back into the thick black fog.

The girl watches him go for a moment. Other destitute figures come up for her attention. She turns from the tree to hand a brightly wrapped present to an old man. He smiles gratefully.

Inside a Garret, the fierce wind blows a flimsy ragged covering from the skylight window, and through the missing or broken panes the icy cold penetrates the room. Lulu, now gone to seed, unkempt and almost in rags, climbs onto a packing-case to nail the rag back over the opening. But first she takes an old, rusty tin pan, which now serves to catch the drops of water which fall through the skylight, and tips it out into the street below. Then she nails the rag back into place.

She goes back into the garret, which is horrifying in its degradation. The only pieces of furniture are a narrow, iron camp bed with a tattered mattress, full of holes which are not covered by any bed-clothes. Before it stands a coarse, wooden table. Next to that, a giant armchair. It must once have been very beautiful. Even now, its indestructible form has a rhythm of shape and lines; but its upholstery and ornament are threadbare and in tatters. Otherwise all there is, is an empty packing-case stood on end near the table.

On the table an old paraffin lamp gives light — it is the kind which is hung up in kitchens or on landings. Its glass is broken and black with soot. There are two or three things more : a cracked plate, a dirty cup, a knife and a piece of stale bread : beside this piece of hard, dry bread, a broken fragment of looking-glass and a comb. Lulu remains standing by the table, wiping the dirt from her hands onto her dress. She lifts up the dimly-burning lamp and sees that it has only a little paraffin left. Giving an ill-tempered shrug, she tries to screw the sooty wick down a little lower.

Alwa is crouched on the bed. He has pressed his back into the corner between the bed-rail and the wall. Over his hunched knees he has spread layers of newspaper. About his shoulders, which are contracted from the cold, he has thrown an old towel. He has hollow cheeks, his eyes dream feverishly. He pays no attention to Lulu.

She has picked up the bread crust from the table and is trying to divide it with the knife. The hardness of the dried-up crust resists her, the knife only slides off it. She throws it back on the table and tries to break the bread apart. After a little effort, she is successful. Without a word, she puts one half aside for Alwa.

He does not move, but only stares at the bread.

Lulu sits down on the packing-case and tries to eat.

Alwa still can do nothing but stare dumbly ahead of him.

Lulu takes a bite, but spits it out almost immediately. It is disgusting. She puts the bread back on the table with a grimace.

The plank door which leads onto the stairway is opened. Schigolch has arrived.

He comes over to the table and sits there. He is apparently unchanged; he has the same cunning face, almost the same stiff round hat with a greasy border. An overcoat bags around his thin body. It is green with age, hangs right down to his ankles and is buttoned up to the throat. We never discover what Schigolch wears under this article of clothing. He fidgets in a pocket and his eyes flash as he triumphantly brings out a bottle and puts it on the table.

Lulu takes little notice of him. (Still on page 114) She leans the piece of looking-glass against the lamp and idly combs her hair.

Sitting in the big chair, Schigolch opens the bottle and takes a deep draught out of it. [He hands it across to Lulu, and she takes a drink too. She is not used to it; it makes her shiver afterwards.]

Then Schigolch pours some of the spirits into the cup and pushes it over to Alwa, standing it beside his untouched piece of bread.

Alwa reaches for the cup and empties it in hurried little gulps.
[Lulu is now curling her hair, while Schigolch tries to warm his hands at the lamp. She chases him away with the tongs.] Having got rid of him, she pushes her face close to the looking-glass and carefully begins to colour her lips with a little end of lipstick.

Now Alwa takes the piece of bread as well. He tries to eat some of it and manages only with difficulty. He laughs to himself, and says bitterly :

TITLE : *It is remarkable that one can get spirits on credit . . . but never bread . . .*

Lulu goes on putting on her lipstick.
She looks at her reflection in the mirror, and instinctively her hand comes up to pat her hair.
She does not notice how Schigolch contemplates her with a cheerful smirk.
Watching her image in the mirror, she rubs her fingers over her lips to even out the colour. Reflected in the mirror, we now see Schigolch's hand come up under her chin.
Taking her under the chin, he says jokingly :

[TITLE : *Why the artistry? We like you as you are!*]

She pushes his hand away and stands up. Schigolch laughs heartily, catches her as she tries to pass him and pulls her onto his knee. Scolding him impatiently, she breaks free.
At this moment, the rag over the skylight bursts apart again and the wind and the wet howl into the room.
Angry and freezing, Lulu looks up at the hole. But this time she does not go to fix it. Instead, she crosses the room to where Alwa is crouched at the head of the bed. (Still on page 115) She snatches the cloth from his shoulders and wraps herself in it.
[Throwing a remark to the two men,] she goes to the door. She stands there a moment, then starts to go out down the stairs.
Alwa gives a startled look after her, pushes the newspapers off his legs and jumps up. He puts his cap on his head and makes as if to follow her, but Schigolch stretches out a hand to hold him back. Excitedly, Alwa protests and argues with the little man.
Breaking free of him, Alwa hurries out onto the landing. Schigolch rushes after him, still trying to stop him. But Alwa is feverishly

determined. (Production Still on page 115) So **Schigolch** gives a philosophical shrug and consents to go out with Alwa after Lulu. He turns up the collar of his coat.

[In the Street outside, the old house door yawns like a toothless mouth in the fog. Somewhat to the side, there are the half-curtained window-panes of a public house. Lulu comes out of the doorway of the house. She stands shivering for a moment, drawing the cloth tightly around her (Still on page 116), then slowly, aimlessly, she goes off to one side. A man passes her and looks into her face. She takes no notice of him, but walks on.]

Now Alwa and Schigolch come out and steal after her.

Before they can reach Lulu, a man has spoken to her near a street-lamp. [Lulu starts to walk on, but the man tramps after her and holds her back. Now she stops.] Alwa hurries up and plants himself protectively beside Lulu. The strange man looks at Alwa, murmurs an apology, touches his hat brim in greeting, and goes on his way. Alwa looks, almost apologetically, into Lulu's eyes.

Now Schigolch is standing there, too. He looks round after the man, then he pushes Alwa to one side [steps up to Lulu and, jovially digging her in the ribs, says with a grin:

TITLE: *Pity . . . I should so much have liked to eat Christmas pudding once more before I die . . .*

He pushes his hat back boldly on his forehead and gives Lulu an encouraging wink.] Then he turns and drags the speechless Alwa away. Lulu stands a moment, alone against the wall of the public house. And all alone, she turns on her heel and walks aimlessly on through the streets. In the glow of the street-lamps swathes of fog drive across her retreating figure. They become thicker and darker . . . then slowly the letters on a large poster grow out of the fog:

NOTICE

To the Women of London

For some time an unknown man has been trying to entice women and girls into dark, out-of-the-way places, and there murder them. Unfortunately, he has succeeded in doing this on four occasions. We therefore warn all women and girls not to go out at night without an escort. The man is described as about 6 feet high, has a sallow complexion, with strikingly narrow shoulders and small, restless eyes.

The Lord Mayor of London

[A shadow falls on the poster and grows as a man steps in front of the warning notice. (Still on page 117) After a brief glance at it, he walks on. Now we can see that it is the strange man whose unusual behaviour struck the young Salvation Army sister so forcibly. He glides through the fog along streets lined with ugly brick houses. At the next bend in the street, he encounters another figure. It is Lulu. He tries to by-pass her, but Lulu bars his way and says something to him. He shakes his head and tries to walk on by pushing her out of his way with both hands. But she seizes his hands and pulls him with her round the corner.]

In the Garret, Schigolch sits in the armchair with his bottle beside him. He seems to be in a cheerful mood which is only spoiled by Alwa, who cannot sit down. He walks up and down the attic like a caged animal. Once, twice, he gives a start, listens for the door. It is nothing, he has deceived himself.

Lulu and the man come up the Stairs. The man's footsteps become slower, more hesitant, until at last he stops altogether. Lulu, who has gone ahead, turns and sees the man trying to turn round and go out again.

He hesitates, a deep conflict raging within him. Lulu stretches out her hand to him.

She pleads for him to come.

The man seems hounded, trapped by something within himself, some force he is desperately trying to break free of.

He looks up at Lulu. At last he forces out the words :

[TITLE : *I have no money!*

Lulu laughs out aloud : ' Is that it ! ' She nestles up to him and pleads :

TITLE : *Come on — I like you!*]

Her face is near to his across the banister. Her big eyes look invitingly at him. Her loosening mouth offers itself to him for a kiss. The muscles of the man's face become stiff and knotted. Unmoving,

131

his eyes stare at the girl, eyes that have become like greedy holes in his tormented face. [Only his right hand moves, jerks backwards into his hip pocket. He pulls out a small dark object.]

A squeeze of his finger makes a knife-blade spring out and stand firm in the handle, sharp and gleaming dully behind his back. (Still on page 118) Then his hand stretches out hugely over the banister; quivering with tension, it at last opens and lets the knife fall far down into the well of the staircase. His back slumps forward in relief. An expression crosses his face like a deliverance. The cramp dissolves, he smiles at Lulu and follows her.

Almost cheerful, the two begin to mount the stairs. Lulu goes ahead, leading the way and pulling the man up behind her.

In the Garret, Schigolch lifts the bottle serenely to his lips.

In his pacings about the room, Alwa's shoulder brushes a rope hanging from the rafters. It is shaped into a noose. He stops by it, and looks steadfastly at it. (Still on page 118)

Schigolch goes on drinking, quite unconcerned. He puts his pipe in his mouth, his beady eyes fixed now on Alwa.

Alwa seems transfixed by the rope suspended before him. Suddenly he gives a start, snatches open the door and listens for the footsteps of the two coming up the stairs.

Schigolch, who has been watching him narrowly, instantly jumps up as Alwa dashes past him. He follows him out of the door.

At the top of the Stairs, Schigolch forces Alwa — who is clinging to the banisters and staring down in the darkness of the stairway — to hurry and hide in a dark corner with him.

For the man and Lulu are already coming up and have eyes only for one another. Lulu opens the door, and they both vanish into the garret. The door has hardly shut when Alwa rushes out of the hiding-place. He stands outside it, shivering. But before his shame can force him to break down the door, Schigolch intervenes. The little man closes his hand across Alwa's mouth and draws him, drags him, feebly protesting, down the stairway.

The man is now sitting in the big armchair in the garret, leaning back at his ease. He seems almost cheerful as he looks up, with calm eyes, at Lulu.

She stands before him. She has taken the cloth from her shoulders, shakes it because it has become damp in the fog outside, and spreads it over the bed-rail to dry. Then she turns her face to the man and they both look at one another.

He smiles and stretches out his hand to her. She comes forward and takes it in hers. With one jump, she springs with both knees into his lap. She lays her hands on his shoulders, while he holds her round her narrow hips. They laugh easily at one another, harmlessly, like children.

On one side of the hall in the house, there is a little door which leads into the public house. Schigolch and Alwa emerge from the passage. Schigolch stops by the door. He sends a little cunning glance up the stairway, then, with a gentlemanly manner, he reaches for the door handle and opens the door. We can see the interior of the public house, where tables and drinkers are illuminated through the thick smoke by the warm orange light of many lamps. Schigolch tries to drag Alwa in with him. But Alwa wrenches himself free with a violent pull and leaves the house by the open street door. Schigolch shrugs his shoulders and enters the public house, closing the door behind him.

In the Garret, the man tries to pull Lulu towards him, so as to kiss her. Lulu playfully defends herself, pushing her arms against his chest. She asks him something. He shakes his head, laughing. She begins to rummage inquisitively in his pockets, smiling happily at him as she does so. He good-humouredly allows her to do it.

In one of the inside pockets of his jacket, she finds the sprig of mistletoe and the little candle which he got from the Salvation Army sister.

She laughs, childishly delighted with this find.

She pulls it out . . .

And looks at it, wonderingly, as if it were something very precious.

He is amused by her naïve pleasure, his eyes gently absorbed in her.

Lulu clasps the mistletoe to her in delight.

He smiles.

Still crouching on his lap, she hunts on the table for one of the matches lying around there. She strikes the match, lights the candle and sticks it, gravely and importantly, on the table in front of them. Then she lays the little sprig of mistletoe before it, moving it once, twice, to get the best effect. (Still on page 119)

The man's eyes are fixed on the table.

He looks down at her hand resting in his, and covers it with his other hand.

133

She smiles solemnly, and comes back into his arms, nestling up to him. He strokes her hair, rather awkwardly, then draws her head down onto his shoulder.

So they sit there, motionless, for a long time, clasping one another closely and staring at the burning candle . . .

The sprig is lying on the table beside it.

Suddenly, something like a smile passes across the man's face.

His hand reaches out for the sprig of mistletoe and picks it up . . . And laughingly he holds it over Lulu's head.

Slyly, Lulu looks up at the mistletoe held quivering in the man's hand, above her head.

The man smiles.

Her eyes question him, a little flirtatiously.

Coming closer to her face, he says :

TITLE : *You're under the mistletoe . . . symbol of redemption and forgiveness . . . now you must let yourself be kissed . . .*

Willingly she shuts her eyes and raises her lips to his. His face bends over hers.

Suddenly the paraffin lamp flares up slightly.

The unexpected little flash of light makes the man raise his eyes. He stops.

He sees the table, where the lamp again flares.

The man's calm, happy expression gives way to fear, the fear becomes a paroxysm. His hands clutch at Lulu's shoulders, tightly, even savagely, while his pupils grow wider and wider as he stares at the table. (Still on page 119)

The sight which fills him with such horror is the bread-knife, lying on the table under the lamp.

The man seems to want to hide his eyes behind Lulu's shoulder. But he is captivated, held by the inescapable reality of the knife.

Its long, pointed blade reflects the flare of the lamp.

The man gasps in terror; no matter what he does, he cannot escape his fate.

The knife glints evilly.

He shakes with terror, biting into Lulu's shoulder in the desperate attempt to stop himself reaching out for the fateful knife.

His breath is coming in short painful gasps now. But the struggle to resist it is too much; he surrenders to his obsession. And surrender

134

is like a release, there is no more agony now. As his hand reaches out, it is only pleasure that he feels. His mouth stays open, his teeth shine under his wide-open lips. Inexorably, his hand reaches across to the knife and clenches round the handle. The blade glints invitingly.

Lulu's face rests innocently in his arms, waiting. Her eyes flicker. The knife blade gleams.

Lulu, in her relaxed abandon, suspects nothing. Her lips part for the anticipated kiss. The man leans over her slowly, easing his body across to cover hers, then, a sharp movement . . . In the darkness, Lulu's body can just be seen behind the man's broad back. She gives a jerk and falls to one side. The man falls with her; slowly her hand loosens its hold on his side. She slips to the floor, her hand flopping lifelessly away.

The lamp flares up once, twice, in quick succession. Hand and knife have vanished. Then the flame goes out and darkness spreads over the table. Only the little candle burns thinly. Its weak flame can illuminate nothing, only somewhere it is reflected as a pale cross.

Outside the House, Alwa is leaning with his shoulders against the wall and looking vacantly into the distance. Suddenly he gives a start and steals a look towards the door of the house. A dark figure steps hastily out of the doorway. The man has his coat buttoned up. With a shiver he turns up the collar. His shoulders hunched, his hands deep in his pockets, he plunges into the fog and gradually disappears into the distance.

Alwa looks after him. He feels a choking sensation in his throat. Weakly, he lets his head fall sideways . . .

And his body moves for comfort to the wall. He presses face and chest against its moist cold. But he cannot prevent the shaking of his shoulders. Alwa gives way, without shame, to a fit of uncontrollable sobbing.

In the Street, the Salvation Army is on the march. The car with the Christmas tree drives in the middle, while the Salvationists march behind their band, playing and singing a solemn chorale. On the metal coils of their wind instruments, a hundred tiny reflections palely gleam . . . all crosses. Out of the fog, they come up the street. Poor creatures stand and watch; others accompany them, children in hand.

In the Public House Bar, burly figures are seated, with two or three

135

prostitutes, round a table. Schigolch is among them, making merry. The Salvation Army come marching down the street, holding high their banners and singing hymns.

The men in the bar listen, and the compulsion of old memories makes them stand up. Caps and hats are respectfully taken off.

The Salvation Army come down the street, and the music swells up again as they all sing:

[TITLE : *Christ is risen* . . .]

And in the bar, when one of the girls picks up the tune and begins to sing, little by little all the others join in.

The Army marches on through the foggy street.

The old Proprietress of the public house comes up with a dish which she puts, with a twinkle in her eye, before Schigolch. He sits down, glances slyly at his singing companions, and then, with quiet enjoyment, begins to eat what he has hoped for — Christmas pudding.

In the Street outside the House, the Salvation Army, still singing and playing, once more begins its march away.

Alwa gazes after it.

And as the figures of the group begin to be obliterated by the fog . . .

Alwa slowly detaches himself from the wall and stands, defeated, for a moment. (Still on page 120) A cruel shaft of light throws his despondent body into relief against the dark wall. He is a pathetic creature. Somehow he draws himself up.

And, as if pulled by some force, he follows the Salvation Army up the street; their figures already disappearing under the arch of a railway bridge. A broken, defeated figure, he stumbles after them, stopping only once to look back at the house. Then he treads slowly, heavily on, till the Salvation Army and he are swallowed up, lost in the fog.

136